# EXODUS
## THE WAY OUT

JOHN N. OSWALT

# EXODUS
## THE WAY OUT

JOHN N. OSWALT

Francis Asbury Press
Distributed by Warner Press
Anderson, Indiana

Warner Press, Inc.
Warner Press and "Warner Press" logo are trademarks of Warner Press, Inc.

*Exodus*
*The Way Out*

Copyright © 2013 John N. Oswalt


All Scripture quotations, unless otherwise indicated, are the author's paraphrase.

Scripture quotations marked NKJV are taken from the New King James Version. Copyright © 1982 by Thomas Nelson, Inc. Used by permission. All rights reserved.

All rights reserved. No part of this publication may be reproduced, stored in a retrieval system, or transmitted in any form or by any means—electronic, mechanical, photocopy, recording or any other—except for brief quotations in printed reviews, without prior written permission of the publisher.

Requests for information should be sent to:
Warner Press Inc
2902 Enterprise Dr
P.O. Box 2499
Anderson, IN 46013
www.warnerpress.org


ISBN (pbk): 978-1-59317-652-5
ISBN (ePub): 978-1-59317-653-2
ISBN (Kindle): 978-1-59317-654-9


Printed in the United States of America.

# Contents

# Acknowledgments

Many people have had a hand in bringing this book to fruition. Pride of place goes to the late Dr. Robert A. Traina, in whose Pentateuch class I sat in 1970. His remarkable insights have shaped my thinking on these books ever since.

This book began in a Bible study offered at Indian Springs Holiness Camp Meeting at Flovilla, Georgia. The staff there kindly recorded the presentation; then Camille Winslow transcribed the recording. Next Peggy Allender edited the transcription. At that point, the material was placed in the files of the Francis Asbury Society in Wilmore, Kentucky.

Eventually, Peggy Allender, office manager, and Mark Royster, director of publications, respectively, for the Francis Asbury Society, persuaded me that I should use the edited transcript as the starting point for this book. I have now done that and Joseph Allison and his staff at Warner Press have encouraged me and assisted in the final preparation. Along the way Jennie Lovell has also given assistance in formatting the manuscript.

To all these and many others, including my wife Karen, I extend my sincerest thanks.

# The Place of Exodus in the Church Today

## Importance of Understanding the Bible Correctly

Is it really important whether we Christians understand the Bible correctly? I mean, the Bible does not save us, Jesus does, so can we not be satisfied with just a minimal knowledge of the Bible?

No, we cannot, because of the distinctive nature of the Christian faith. We believe that God has revealed his nature and his will for human life in the pages of the Bible. Therefore, the Bible is just as important to us as a chart and a compass are to a sailor. It is not enough for the sailor to have a chart and compass; he also has to be able to read and interpret them correctly. If he does not know that those particular marks on the chart show a reef just underwater, extending far out from a certain point of land, then all the sailor's sincerity and good intentions will not prevent him from ripping the bottom out of his boat when he sails across that reef. That is the way it is with Christians and the Bible: It is not enough just to have a Bible. We need to know what Scripture means for us as we live our daily lives or we may well find that we have constructed for ourselves an understanding of God that has no reality at all. That is also why we need to know all of the Bible and not just the last quarter of it.

## The Importance of the Old Testament

When people find out that I teach the Old Testament, they often ask me why that's necessary. After all, we are Christians, and the New Testament is our book; the Old Testament is a Jewish book, is it not? The short answer to that question is that the whole Bible is our Book. Really? There were no Christians around when the Old Testament was written. No, but the Holy Spirit was! Since the Holy Spirit inspired the writing from Genesis to Malachi, we can believe that Jesus and the Church were in his mind, whether the inspired human writers understood the implications of what they were writing or not. This is the very point that the early Christian leaders fought out. In the end, they were convinced that the whole Bible is about Christ and that if we are to understand the gospel correctly, we have to read the whole book. Who of us would read the last chapter of *War and Peace* and then claim that we had read the book? None of us. Yet that is how many of us propose to read the Bible. The result is that too many times we have badly misunderstood that last quarter of the Bible, the New Testament. For instance, some of us think the Bible teaches that salvation consists of having our sins forgiven and being given a guarantee of heaven. That is not true, as the first three-quarters of the Book makes plain.

Several years ago, Karen and I acted as our own contractors in building a new house. I discovered quickly that we could not start with the second floor. It is hard to keep those boards up in the air long enough to nail them together! A builder always starts with the foundation, and then adds the first floor. That is what the Old Testament provides for us: it is the foundation and the first floor of our understanding of God, so that when we come to the second floor—the New Testament—we will understand just what Jesus and the apostles are telling us.

So how does the Old Testament help us to understand and interpret the New? First of all, it provides essential background and theological foundations for New Testament teachings. The New Testament writers assumed that their readers would know the Old Testament, so they did not attempt to go back and make those points again when they said something about divine and human reality.

The New Testament writers assume that we have learned about the majesty of God—his tremendous glory and otherness, his wonder. So the New Testament can focus on his nearness. He is near, nearer than breathing. But it is still the almighty Majesty who is near, not some friendly little elf who exists to make our prayers come true.

The New Testament writers assume we have learned about the justice of God: In short, if you sin, you will die. If you break the law of God, you will break yourself upon it. So the New Testament writers can focus their efforts on telling us about the God of grace, who in response to his just law gives himself as a sacrifice for us all.

The New Testament writers assume that their readers have already learned about the holiness of God: that God is morally perfect, the one in whom is no spot or blemish, the one who is true and right and pure. So they can tell us about his forgiveness—that a person like you or me can walk into the presence of the Holy God and not be destroyed.

But what if we do not know the Old Testament, the first three-quarters of our Book? What if we only understand the message of the New Testament and conclude that God is very near and gracious and forgiving? There is a great danger that we will assume that God is a kind, friendly, and useful Pal. We are tempted to visualize him as an indulgent great-grandpa in the sky whose habit is to pat us on the head and say, "Oh, that's all right, honey. It doesn't really matter; you can do whatever you want."

This is happening in the Christian church in the United States today; as we have progressively lost the Old Testament, we have made God smaller and smaller and smaller. We imagine him as our servant, who says, "I forgive you, no matter what you do or where you do it or how you do it." But the New Testament writers did not mean that. They said, "Oh, think of it! The Holy God, the almighty God, the terrible God, the God of justice and truth and glory—that God says, 'I forgive you.' That cosmic God has come near to us in love and grace and mercy." So God is not diminished as we read the whole Bible, but rather his greatness is enriched.

### The Big Question

But the Old Testament is not merely background and theological foundation for the New Testament: it tells us the questions that the New Testament is answering. As in the game of *Jeopardy*, we need to know what the questions are if we are to understand the true meaning of the answers. There is one great question that the Old Testament proposes and which the New Testament gloriously answers: "How can a sinful, mortal, finite human being ever live in the presence of, and share the character of, a morally perfect, eternal, infinite God?" That is the overarching question from Genesis to Malachi. The Old Testament does not ask, "How can my sins be forgiven so that

I can be assured of going to heaven?" References to forgiveness appear infrequently in the Old Testament and heaven hardly at all. Why is that? Because these are not central to its message. The fact is that we were created to walk with God and that only those who are actually like him in his behavior can do so (see Eph 1:4). But it is also clear that we don't naturally share the revealed character of God and, in fact, don't seem to be able to do that, despite our best efforts. There is something badly wrong with us (see Gen 6:5), something that must be corrected if we are to have any chance of becoming what we were made for. Thus, the question for every human being that ever lived or will live is this: How can I, deeply flawed as I am, share the character of the holy God and thus live forever in his presence as I was created to do? And it is this question that the cross (including resurrection and Pentecost) can answer.

I am not saying that forgiveness is unimportant or that eternal life is of no consequence! Forgiveness is essential to our having a right relationship with God, and heaven is the natural and expected consequence of that relationship. But forgiveness is not an end in itself, as North American evangelicalism has tended to make it. Forgiveness ushers us into the transforming relationship with God, which is the real purpose of what God has done for us. And heaven is not a goal to attain after we die. It is the eternal perpetuation of the life in God that he invites us to experience here and now.

So the Old Testament shows us the question to which the New Testament provides the definitive answer. However, the Old Testament does not merely pose the question. It explores and develops the question in ways that help us to understand the true shape of that final answer. So, if we want a proper understanding of the biblical doctrine of salvation, we must start with the

Old Testament. If we were to start with a section of the New Testament—say, Romans—to formulate our doctrine of salvation, there is a better-than-even chance that we will misinterpret the truth of that great epistle. But if we see its truths in the light of the Old Testament, we will read it correctly and see it in the proper light.

Nowhere is the subject of salvation dealt with more clearly than in the book of Exodus. This book is in many ways the key treatment in the whole Bible for understanding this truth. Just as Genesis is the key book for understanding origins (e.g., the origin of the universe, the origin of our faith), Exodus is the key book for understanding salvation. It reveals the true nature of our problem: Why is it that human beings need salvation? From what do we need to be saved? What is the human side of the problem? How does God overcome what we have done? And what does salvation bring us to, in the end? The answers to these questions and many more are all to be found in Exodus.

## Truth in the Context of Narrative

The treatment of salvation in Exodus is all the more powerful because it is told in the context of narrative. Mahatma Ghandi reportedly told his friend, American missionary E. Stanley Jones, that he did not believe the Bible was divine because it was composed largely of stories. Apparently, he thought that divine revelation should take the form of bare, contextless pronouncements, as the Koran or many of the Hindu holy books do. But we believe the Bible is divinely inspired, not in spite of large sections in narrative form, but precisely because it appears in such a form. Yahweh does not sit in lonely isolation in heaven hurling instructions at us. These would be largely meaningless. Instead, he has stepped into our context of time and space and has revealed himself in relationship to what we know and see and experience.

This is the genius of narrative: It teaches from within the life of the disciple. In so doing, it underlines the great truth that time and space are not illusory reflections cast up by the endlessly turning wheel of existence (as many other religions teach). No, time and space are real creations of the one God, and what we do in them has real consequences.

## Two Key Themes in Exodus

### Covenant

Before we begin to look at the book of Exodus in detail, I want to highlight two important themes the book addresses. The first is covenant. This one term is so definitive of biblical faith that Christians call the two parts of the Bible "old covenant" and "new covenant." Every time we celebrate Communion, we hear those words, "This is the new covenant in my blood." What does this word *covenant* mean, and why is it so central to our faith?

An English-language dictionary may say that the words *covenant* and *contract* are synonymous, but the biblical covenant is far more than a contract. It involves two parties committing themselves to each other without reservation. That is what God does in regard to you and me. The eternal, omnipotent, majestic, infinite, holy God binds himself to you and me without reservation. What an amazing thought! He does not need to do that. He does not need us to do anything for him. Yet God gives himself to us in covenant. When we talk about salvation or the nature of eternal life, we are talking about a covenant between God and humanity. Its nature and content are clearly laid out for us in the book of Exodus.

*Holiness: The Goal of Salvation*

The second overarching concept of the book of Exodus is personal holiness. Here we encounter one of the tragedies of Christendom, especially in its modern North American form. American Christians have come to believe that God offers salvation to everybody but holiness (if it is granted by God at all) only to a select few. That is untrue, tragically untrue, and many of the conditions in the church today are the result of our acceptance of this untruth.

Consider this: What is salvation about, in its full biblical sense? Salvation is about God's delivering us from the dung heap of our sin, cleansing us of that sin, and bringing us home blameless into his holy presence. Salvation is about being made into the character and the shape of God, which is what holiness is. The very idea that we can be saved to continue in sin is a heresy, and Exodus makes that crystal clear. Exodus teaches us that we cannot separate salvation from holiness. Holiness is impossible apart from gracious divine deliverance, and deliverance that does not issue in genuine personal holiness is a miscarriage of grace.

CHAPTER 1

# Exodus: Structure and Content

## The Way Out

*The Way Out of Physical Bondage*

The title of the book, *Exodus*, is a Greek word meaning "the way out." When we ask, "The way out of what?," the answer seems deceptively simple. Obviously, it is the story of how Israel found its way out of Egypt. Exodus is about the exodus!

But think again. How much of the book is about getting out of Egypt? Hardly more than a third. The Hebrews are out of Egypt by chapter 15, but there are forty chapters in the book. So we have to ask again, "Exodus is about the way out of what?" Is it possible that Israel had some deeper problem than physical bondage from which they needed to be delivered? This is not to suggest that physical bondage and suffering are not real problems, or that God was not really concerned about them. But if and when people are delivered from physical slavery, we cannot assume that their deepest problems have been solved. What are these problems?

*The Way Out of Spiritual Darkness*

If we look into the book of Exodus carefully, we find a statement repeated in one form or another nearly a dozen times in chapters

6–14. In the Bible, as in life, repetition is a primary means of emphasis, so this statement must highlight an important point. The statement is, "Then he/they/you will know that I am Yahweh" (e.g., 6:7). Physical bondage is not the Israelites' primary problem. No, the primary problem is spiritual darkness. They do not know God. This problem burns upon the heart of God as he looks at the world today and sees such suffering, shame, tragedy, pain, and oppression. His fatherly heart bleeds; he wants to set people free from their spiritual darkness. Do not imagine that he looks at the masses living under bondage today and does not care. The fact is, he has an even deeper concern than shackles and instruments of torture: "They do not know me, and they need to know me." In many ways, physical suffering and bondage are the result of this deeper problem. When we do not know God, we become the victims of our physical circumstances. What you and I need above all else is to know Yahweh, the One who brought all things into existence and the One upon whom all existence depends.

Do you ever listen to what Christians typically say at prayer meetings? I confess I do, and sometimes I am a little embarrassed. "Lord, if you would just get so-and-so over being sick." "Lord, if you would just deliver so-and-so from drug addiction." "Lord, if you would just get so-and-so out of financial trouble. Their car broke down in the middle of nowhere and they had to take it to so-and-so's garage." (As though God did not already know that!)

What are we really saying in these kinds of prayers? We are saying, "Lord, if you would just save us from our circumstances, everything would be all right." Would it? Not necessarily.

That is the kind of prayer the Hebrew people prayed: "O God, just get us out of Egypt and then you can let us alone. Just get us out of Egypt and we can take care of it from there on. Our big problem, God, is these Egyptian taskmasters who beat us up. If you would just deliver us from them, that's all we ask."

But God says, in effect, "You ask too little. Physical suffering is not your real problem. Your real problem, child, is that you don't know me. You don't know who I am. You don't know what I want to do in your life."

How easily we pray, "Lord, deliver me out of my trouble," when the Lord is saying, "Don't you understand what this trouble is about? It's an opportunity for you to know me."

Instead, we should be asking, "O Lord, what do you want me to learn through this trouble, this tragedy? O Lord, grant that I may not get out of this without learning everything you have for me in it." Do you ever pray that way? Too often I do not. Instead of saying, "Lord, let me know you in this time of trouble like I have never known you before," I tend to say, "Lord, just get me out of this!"

I am not suggesting that God sends us trouble just to teach us things. I do not suppose that God sits in heaven and periodically says, "Well, Gabriel, doesn't Oswalt need a broken leg about now? That might straighten him out, don't you think?" That is not the God we worship.

But I do believe this: Nothing happens to us without God's knowledge and permission. This means nothing happens to us that God cannot sanctify and turn to good purpose in our lives. We can live with confidence in that fact. No, I don't know why a certain misfortune happened to me, but I do know that it happened with my Father's permission. And since it did, he can use it for my blessing.

That is what happened to the Hebrews. Think what would have happened if they had never gone into captivity. We would not have had the Exodus story. They would never have learned what they learned about God in the wilderness. So do I think that God sent them to Egypt so they would be enslaved and he could demonstrate his power to deliver them? Never! He sent them into Egypt to save them from the famine that was about to overwhelm them (Gen 50:20). Captivity came upon them because of the tyranny of the Pharaohs. God did not cause their trouble, but because it came, God was able to accomplish a greater good and they were able to learn some things about God that they might not have learned in any other way. Exodus was their way out. The way out of bondage, yes—but so much more than that! God showed them the way out of spiritual darkness, the way into truth, the way of a life-transforming relationship with their Creator.

So what did God reveal to the Hebrews that enlightened that spiritual darkness?

In chapters 1–15, we see a stunning revelation of God's power. But it was not enough to know that God was able to deliver them from captivity. They had to wonder, Who is God? What kind of person is this, anyway? Who has delivered us? "Then you will know that I am God," he had promised. But even after they had escaped Pharaoh's army, they wondered what God was like.

God replies, "I thought you would never ask. Let me show you."

Thus, in chapters 16–24, the second main section of the book, we have a twofold revelation of the character and nature of God. The first is found in chapters 16–18, where God's providence is revealed. Again and again, God demonstrates that he cares about the basic needs of his people, about water and food and protection. He is a compassionate God.

In chapters 19–24, we find another aspect of God's character and nature: He is a God of principles. Through the Sinai Covenant, God invites his people to learn his character and nature by living according to his principles. It is as though God says, "Do you want to know what I am like? All right, live my life. Obey my laws. Value what I value." Act in obedience to God's covenant requirements and you will know what kind of God he is, because those requirements express his character.

In my graduate work, I studied Egyptian religious literature of the New Kingdom (ca. 1550–1200 BC). As I was doing that, I kept one eye on the Bible, thinking that I would like to compare what the Egyptians believed about God with what the Hebrews believed about God. Well, I found that the two were as different as day and night. This difference was not merely in their respective theologies, but in their whole approach to the natural world. The Egyptian religious literature discusses what the god is made of, where he came from, who his mother is, what his relations are with the other gods, and so on. There is nothing of that sort in the Bible, absolutely nothing. What do you have instead? A narrative of God's involvement in the lives of a very specific group of people, culminating in his providing them a code of law. I thought, "Wait a minute, what is going on here?" And then it dawned on me: God was saying, "You can't name me; you can't know what I am made of; you can't know what I look like; you can't know what I wear, none of that. But do you want to know the kind of person I am? Then live my life; act like I act."

So Yahweh the Covenant Lord says, "Don't bear false witness about your neighbor." And Abe says, "All right. That's no problem." Then the day comes when it is to Abe's advantage to twist the truth a little bit about Zeke; it will make Zeke look bad and it will make Abe look good. But Abe remembers his promise to God, and does not do it.

All of a sudden, Abe says, "Wait a minute here, wait. Do you suppose God is like that with me? Do you suppose my reputation is safe in God's hands? Do you suppose God can be trusted with all that I am and he won't twist me or abuse me?"

So God elbows Gabriel and says, "I believe he is getting it. I believe he is getting it." The Hebrews are learning the character of God by living it out.

## The Way Out of Alienation from God

So when we come to the end of Exodus 24, God has delivered his people from two problems: the problem of physical bondage and (at least in principle) the problem of spiritual darkness. The book has shown the way out of two grievous problems in which the Hebrews had been living. So the narrative has come to its end, has it not?

Well, no, as a matter of fact. There are still sixteen chapters to go. Was there a still deeper problem for which God wanted to provide a way of escape? What more could there be beyond those? To answer that question, we need to look at the content of those remaining chapters.

These chapters are all about the tabernacle, and the information is not very palatable to us modern readers. First, chapters 25–31 give us a set of very detailed instructions about how the tabernacle is to be built, what its furniture is to be, what its priests are to wear in it, and so on. Then we find in chapters 35–40 a report of how these instructions were followed. That report is almost a verbatim repetition of the instructions themselves, with just the pronouns and verb tenses changed ("you shall make"... "he made"). What is going on here, and why are we told the same thing twice?

We are on the way to answering our question if we compare God's situation at the end of chapter 24 and at the end of chapter 40. At the end of chapter 24, God resides on the mountain where only Moses could go. At the end of chapter 40, he is present in the tabernacle in the very center of the camp. "Then the cloud covered the tabernacle and the glory of the Lord filled the tabernacle" (Ex 40:35). The tabernacle is about the presence of God, and its construction demonstrates that God has come home to his people.

Here is the greatest problem of all. Do we need deliverance from the suffering that is endemic to a sin-sick world? Oh, yes. Do we need deliverance from our ignorance of the nature and character of our Creator? Oh, yes. But most of all, do we need to escape our alienation from God and from his life, an alienation that is at the heart of the other two? Oh, yes, yes! Exodus occurred, not just to get Hebrews out of Egypt, nor to reveal the glorious truth of God's nature in his providence and in the covenant. Oh, no, the purpose of the Exodus was far greater than that. The Exodus occurred so that God could come home!

Ever since Genesis 3, God had been finagling a way to come home. As that first couple went down a briar-strewn path toward the angels with flaming swords, the devil said, "Admit it, God. I have beaten you. You made them for love and fellowship, but you can never have fellowship with them again. Sin has made them filthy, rotten, defiled. So eat your heart out. I have defeated you."

But God said, "Satan, this is not over. The story has just begun."

The rest of the Bible is about God's coming home to the human heart, God's taking up residence among us. It is easy for us to think that we need what God can do for us, but without God's presence, all of his gifts are worthless. This is what makes Abraham's offering of Isaac so profound. The patriarch is saying, "If it comes to a choice between God and his gifts, I must have God!"

So at the end of the book of Exodus, we hear God saying, "I want to live in your midst; I want to be with you." We see that the final and greatest deliverance of Exodus is from the alienation that is the inevitable result of our self-centered, self-willed existence. So the tabernacle is an indelible picture of the glory of God in the heart of the believer.

Now we know that the tabernacle wasn't the final end of God's story with us. God didn't just mean to live with us; he means to live in us through the Holy Spirit, made available to us in the cross and resurrection. But these final chapters of Exodus point the way to the achievement of that ultimate goal.

What is to be done about the sin that alienated us from God in the first place? It cannot be simply ignored. "The soul that sins shall die" (Ezek 18:4); that is a truth as immutable as gravity. Until that sentence of death was dealt with, nothing else could go forward. Jesus accomplished this on his cross. By becoming "the Lamb of God that takes away the sin of the world" (John 1:29), Christ delivered us from the condemnation and punishment for sin that held us captive and kept God from dwelling in us. But that clause "takes away the sin" must not be overlooked: We are delivered from death and hell in order that God's character may be reproduced in us, all to the end that God may take up residence in us (see Eph 3:14–19).

The wonder of this plan is pictured for us in the splendor and beauty of the tabernacle. Furthermore, the double telling of the tabernacle's construction conveys how important the reality is to God. When we look at that structure in all its beauty—its gold and silver, its purple and blue and red, the sweet smell of incense—we catch a glimpse of how our hearts should look when God resides within us. Pentecost is about the achievement of the true purpose and meaning of the tabernacle.

So we have in Exodus 1–15 a revelation of God's power; in chapters 16–24, a revelation of God's providence and principles;

in chapters 25–40, a revelation of God's presence. The way out of bondage? Yes. The way out of ignorance? Yes. The way out of spiritual alienation? Yes. A way out of separation and loneliness, a way out of fear, a way into the Holy of Holies and the very presence of God? Yes, yes, yes. In the end, that is what the book of Exodus is all about.

## The Historical and Cultural Background

Now that we have some sense of the flow of thought in the book, we need to consider something else in preparation for our study. Many times people say that they find the Old Testament hard to understand. And it is. Why?

To a large extent, it is because the Old Testament is so explicitly tied to the history and the culture of its times. Unless you understand a bit about that history and culture, it is hard to know what is going on. (Actually, the New Testament is rooted in the history and culture of its times too, and it can be much more meaningful if you know something about that history and culture. But the linkage between Scripture and secular culture is not quite as tight there.) You need to know something about the background of the ancient Near East if you are to understand the Old Testament. You don't need a PhD in biblical history or anything on that level, but you should have some basic study tools to find your way. A good study Bible (and it is hard to find a bad one) can help a great deal.

So what do we need to know about the background to the book of Exodus? The Exodus occurred about 1400 BC, fourteen hundred years before Christ.[1] Abraham is thought to have lived

---

1. This date is debated, with some scholars arguing that it happened about 1275 BC, but the essential background is the same.

about two thousand years before Christ, six hundred years earlier. During most of that millennium, 2000–1000 BC, Egypt was the great power in the whole ancient world. The Egyptians' sense of power only added to the complacency that their physical location promoted. Their climate is remarkably stable. The average temperature year-round is 72 degrees Fahrenheit and the sun shines an average of 363 days a year. Before the construction of the Aswan High Dam in the 1960s, the Nile flooded during the same week on the calendar each summer. The flood would recede a few weeks later, again during the same week each year. Not only was the timing of the flood entirely predictable, so was its extent. Far up the river valley, the Nile poured through a narrow canyon. Flood-stage measurements were painted on the wall of this canyon and careful records were kept, correlating the height of the flood waters with how far those waters would spread out when they reached the wide, fertile valley hundreds of miles downstream. So when the flood reached its crest in the canyon, swift messengers were dispatched to tell the valley-dwellers what the extent of the flood would be that year.

With such a pleasant and favorable situation, you can understand why the Egyptians were concerned about the next life. They worried that heaven might not be as good as Egypt! They were preoccupied with funeral practices and preparations simply because they wanted to ensure the continuation of their good life in the next world. Added to all this, their Pharaoh was god incarnate. He protected them and provided everything they needed. So the Egyptians thought the world was their apple. Into this idyllic world, Abraham, Isaac, Jacob, and their descendants came.

## Semitic Rulers of Northern Egypt

It appears that Jacob's family came into Egypt at about the time when Semites, people from Palestine, were actually ruling the delta region of northern Egypt. They had adopted all the customs and prejudices of the Egyptians—its supposedly superior culture—but they were still more favorable to having people from Canaan settle in their land than the native Egyptians ever were. Thus, it is not too surprising that the Bible tells us the Pharaoh was willing to have a Semite be his second-in-command, and invited the Hebrews to settle in the rich land of the delta.

## Semitic Rulers Expelled

But there came a time when native Egyptians rose up and threw out these foreign rulers, and it seems likely that this was when Jacob's descendants found themselves no longer honored guests. Instead, they were considered a positive danger to the state. This expulsion of the foreign rulers ushered in Egypt's last period of greatness, from 1500 to 1200 BC. During this time, the Pharaoh was a military dictator with absolute power. For centuries, the Egyptians had been somewhat paranoid about their northern border at the Sinai Peninsula. All of the other borders—on the south, east, and west—were relatively secure because they had natural barriers to invasion. But the Sinai had no natural defenses, and the riches of Egypt were always a tempting target for those living in Canaan and father east and north. The pharaohs in this last period of greatness decided that the best defense was a good offense, so they moved to control not only the Sinai Peninsula but also the entire eastern Mediterranean coast as far north as they could. In the light of that strategy, it is easy to understand why the Egyptians felt uneasy about a group of Semites living right inside the Sinai borders.

We can also understand, given the Pharaoh's understanding of himself, why Moses sounded so ridiculous when he came to him and said, "I am from God." The Pharaoh would have said, "Oh, really? I don't know you, and I am God." Much of the struggle that goes on in the first part of the book of Exodus is focused on resolving this problem: Pharaoh is not God, any more than you are or I am.

That has always been the human problem: We each think we are God, so we presume to decide what is right and wrong for ourselves. We think we can do whatever we want with our lives. So the great struggle in the human heart is to admit what Pharaoh had to say, "There is One who is greater than I." I saw a poster some time ago that I really liked. It said,

There are two steps to spiritual enlightenment:
1. There is a God.
2. You are not he.

That is what the Pharaoh had to understand, and you can see how difficult that was. The absolute ruler of this wonderful, lush country is confronted by these stupid Semites—many of whom have been kicked out, the rest of whom have been subjected to slavery—who have the nerve to tell him that he is not God. In that setting, that situation, the narrative of Exodus unfolds. Here is the outline that we will be following:

I.   Deliverance: Revelation of Yahweh's Power
     (1:1 –15:21)
     A.   Preparation for deliverance (1:1–6:30)
          1. The need for deliverance (1:1–22)
          2. The preparation of the deliverer (2:1–25)

3. The call of the deliverer (3:1–4:27)

   4. The offer of deliverance (4:28–5:21)

   5. Deliverance: issues clarified (5:22–6:30)

 B. The events of deliverance (7:1–14:31)

   1. The plagues (7:1–12:36)

   2. The crossing of the sea (12:37–14:31)

 C. The song of the sea (15:1–21)

II. The Wilderness: Revelation of Yahweh's Providence (15:22–18:27)

 A. Provision of water (15:21–27)

 B. Provision of food (16:1–36)

 C. Provision of water (17:1–7)

 D. Provision of security (17:8–16)

 E. Provision of organization (18:1–27)

III. The Covenant: Revelation of Yahweh's Principles (19:1–24:18)

 A. Preparation for the covenant (19:1–25)

 B. The terms of the covenant (20:1–23:33)

   1. Commitments of the people (20:1–23:19)

    a. Summary: the Ten Commandments (20:1–17)

    b. Details (20:18–23:19)

   2. Commitments of Yahweh (23:20–33)

 C. Sealing of the covenant (24:1–18)

IV The Tabernacle: Revelation of Yahweh's Person (25:1–40:38)

 A. Instructions for building (25:1–31:18)

 B. Golden calf (32:1–34:35)

 C. Report of building (35:1–40:38)

# Questions for Personal Study or Discussion

1.  What is the approximate date of the events of Exodus, according to Dr. Oswalt? How long was this after the time of Abraham?

2.  What three major problems do the Hebrew people face at the beginning of Exodus?

3.  Dr. Oswalt says that all of the Bible after the garden of Eden story is about God's coming home—to what?

4.  Imagine you are one of the Hebrew slaves in Egypt. How do you feel about Moses' invitation to follow him? (Remember, you don't know Moses. You don't know where he is taking you. After your people's four hundred years under oppression, you hardly know the God that Moses says he is following.)

5.  Recall a time when God invited you to step into the unknown. How did you feel about that? How did you decide what to do?

# CHAPTER 2

# The Need for Deliverance and the Preparation of the Deliverer (Exodus 1–2)

The opening section of Exodus, chapters 1–6, describes God's preparation for deliverance. The section contains five parts: the need for deliverance (ch 1); preparation of the deliverer (ch 2); the call of the deliverer (chs 3–4); the offer of deliverance (ch 5); deliverance itself, and the issues clarified (ch 6).

## The Need for Deliverance

The opening words of Exodus 1 break into the middle of the Old Testament's historical narrative. There is no stage setting, but the author assumes we have read the book of Genesis. "Now these are the names of the children of Israel [Who is that?] that came to Egypt [From where? Why?]. Each man and his household came with Jacob [Who is Jacob? Is he the same as the Israel of the previous sentence?]." We know the answer to all of these questions if we have read the book of Genesis. Apparently, Exodus assumes that we have, and that we know what Genesis is about.

So what is the book of Genesis about? From chapter 12 onward, Genesis is about the promises of God. In a series of conversations, he tells a man and a woman, "I am going to bless you. I am going to give you a child."

They respond, "But we are old."

He replies, "Never mind. I am also going to give you land."

"But Lord, we don't own anything."

"Never mind. I am going to make your descendants more than the stars of the heavens."

"Lord, have you counted the stars recently?"

"Never mind" (see Gen 12:1–3; 15:1–6; 17:1–22).

God came to Abraham and Sarah with these three promises. They were unsolicited and, on the surface, quite unlikely. But the rest of the book of Genesis is the story of the unfolding of these promises through four successive generations, culminating in the provision of sustenance for the descendants of Abraham in Egypt when the whole region was in the grip of famine.

The story continues in the book of Exodus with the great question being addressed again: Can God keep his promises? Now the issue had become even more stark than it had been for Abraham and Sarah. Far from owning the land of Canaan, the descendants of Abraham were slaves in a foreign land. Furthermore, the Pharaoh was attempting to destroy them as a nation, in which case Abraham would end up with no descendants at all. So God's faithfulness was on the line. His truthfulness was on the line. "Wait a minute, God," the Hebrews must have said. "You promised to bless us. You promised us all of these wonderful things, and, God, we are slaves. Will you keep your promises?"

God's answer in Exodus is, "Yes, yes, yes."

Perhaps you have asked that sort of question in your own life: Will God keep his promises to me? Will God keep his promises to the church? Can God keep the marvelous promises he has made to all of his people in the Word? When we look at the situation of our world today, we might be moved to ask, "How can God possibly keep his promises in the midst of this?"

To all of these questions, I think God would say, "Have you read Exodus recently?"

In Exodus 1:1–7, the who of the problem is established. Verse six paints a dark picture: "But Joseph died, all his brothers, all that generation" (NKJV). These are the people that came down to Egypt, they all died. Jacob had died; Jacob's sons had died; a whole generation had died. So had God's promise died with them? No. Here is verse seven: "But the children of Israel were fruitful, and increased abundantly, multiplied and grew exceedingly mighty, and the land was filled with them" (NKJV). Did God keep his promise to multiply the descendants of Abraham? Yes. A whole generation of pioneers had died, but they left behind thousands like them, and these thousands of Jacob's descendants needed deliverance.

In verses 8–22, we are introduced to the what of the problem. The new king in Egypt decided to enslave this large group of Semites who were living just inside his northern border. But look at verse 12: "The more they afflicted them, the more they multiplied and grew. And they [the Egyptians] were in dread of the children of Israel" (NKJV). That experience reminds us of Jacob's life, doesn't it? For ten years, his father-in-law Laban had tricked him, abused him, and misused him. But the more he did, the richer Jacob grew. Trouble is not our problem. God can keep his promises in spite of trouble. So the more the Hebrews were oppressed, the more their numbers increased. Finally, the Egyptians said, "All right, obviously oppression isn't going to do this. We have destroyed them as a people." So in Exodus 1:15–22, we read that the Pharaoh instructed the midwives to kill every boy baby that was born to the Israelites. Hebrew girls would be left alive to intermarry with Egyptians, but there would be no boys to carry on the family line of Abraham.

However, the Pharaoh did not take account of the courage and devotion of the Hebrew midwives (1:17). The great Pharaoh came up against two unimportant midwives. (Of course, there were many more than two, given the large number of the Hebrew people; but two are named as representative of all of them.) These two women had no power, no position, and no status. Yet when the mighty Pharaoh said, "You kill every boy baby of the Hebrews," they wouldn't do it. Why not? Verse 17 says they would not because they feared God. They were more afraid of God than they were of Pharaoh.

I believe the Western church has lost its fear of God. We are not afraid to disobey him anymore. We are not afraid to break his heart. We are not afraid to drag his name in the mud. We believe that couplet from a popular song of the sixties:

> Though it makes Him sad to see the way we live,
> He'll always say, "I forgive."[1]

No! He is not an indulgent god. He is the holy God. He is the One who holds our lives in the palm of his hand. He is the One before whose bar of justice every human being who has ever lived and died will stand one day. But we don't seem to worry about that.

These two Hebrew ladies did worry. They thought, *Maybe Pharaoh can kill us, but we are not afraid of that. We are afraid of standing before God one day and saying, "Yes, God, we disobeyed you. Yes, God, we gave away your promises. Yes, we killed innocent children*

---

1. "He." Lyrics and music by Richard Mullan and John Richards. © EMI Music Publishing.

*because we feared what the Pharaoh might do to us."* So they obeyed God rather than man.

What would happen if a group of people experienced a renewal of the fear of God? I am not talking about a trembling, cowering obeisance before an arbitrary monster who might suddenly lash out at us in an unexpected way. That is not the fear of God. The fear of God is clean (Ps 19:9). Genuine fear of God says, "Lord, I will obey you, I will live for you, I will follow your path because you alone are God. You alone are the Lord. You alone hold my life in your hands, so I will serve you and not fear anyone else." That is the great thing the fear of God does for you: If you fear him, you don't have to fear anything else (Ps 34:4, 11–14).

So the Hebrew midwives weren't afraid of Pharaoh, and I think Pharaoh knew that. Notice that he says: "Why haven't you done this thing?" Why haven't you weak, insignificant, unimportant people rushed to obey me? (Ex 1:15–18). Because they "feared the Lord" (v 17). In a real sense, the whole outcome of the book of Exodus is summed up right there. The Hebrews did not fear Pharaoh and did not obey him, because he was not God. There was still a kernel of faith in the Hebrew people, so God had something to work with, something to build a nation upon. From that kernel would grow a vast, fruitful tree. As a result, we do not know that Pharaoh's name, but we do know the names of those two midwives!

So chapter 1 has established the need for deliverance. It has told us who is in need of deliverance: the descendants of Jacob, who is a descendant of Abraham (1–7). It has also told us why there is a need for deliverance: Not only are these people enslaved in a foreign land, but there is a move afoot to wipe them out as a people (8–21). So this is an exclusively human problem, right? Slavery and genocide are human problems. But no, these are not exclusively human problems. The need for deliverance is also a divine problem. God made promises to give this people a land, and if they are wiped out as a people while enslaved in Egypt, then the God of Abraham is not God at all. In the same way, our slavery to sin and the resultant eternal death is not merely our problem. It is God's problem too. He made us to lavish his love upon, to live in eternal fellowship with, to share his character with. So, as strange as it sounds, God needs to deliver us if he is to accomplish his cosmic creation purposes (see Eph 1:4–6).

## The Preparation of the Deliverer

Chapter 2 of Exodus is about the preparation of the deliverer. This narrative captures my imagination due to its narrowing of focus. Apart from the incident of the midwives, chapter 1 paints the picture of Israel's need in rather broad and general terms. But now the focus narrows from an entire nation to a single couple: "And a man of the house of Levi went and took as wife a daughter of Levi" (2:1 NKJV). That is exactly what the book of Genesis does. In Genesis 1–7, we are introduced to the cosmic problem of sin. Then in Genesis 12:1 we read "Now the LORD had said to Abram..." (NKJV). The narrative's focus shifts from a worldwide problem to a single man. What's the significance of that? Just this: God's salvation is never by means of some broad, impersonal program; it is a personal transaction. God knows your name and mine. Individuals generally have little value in the Eastern world, whereas in the Western world, individual freedom and accountability are primary values. Do you know what accounts for the difference? It is the Bible. If the Bible were lost from our culture, individual worth and accountability would go with it (something we can see happening in our nation already).

God did not devise some vast political or military strategy to deliver his people from bondage. Instead, he chose to use a baby—a creature so helpless that he could not exist for long away from his mother's breast, a baby so vulnerable that his parents had to hide him in a basket, in a swamp.

"Wait a minute, God," you may say. "You don't understand the problem here. Egypt was the greatest military power in the world, and they had a systematic program of ethnic destruction."

God would reply, "You don't understand. It is not a question of what mighty program I can devise. Rather, the question is whether there is a person I can use—one person through whom all of my power can flow."

God says the same thing to you and me when we are tempted to resist his calling. "Oh, I am just one," we protest. "I don't count. I don't matter."

But God says, "You are worth eternity to me; you are worth the cross to me. You, you. Your name is written in blood on my hand. You matter to me, and I can accomplish incredible things if you let me work through you."

So when a Levite man married a woman, salvation for the Hebrew people—for all of us—rested on that decision. This is the glory of God, who uses the weak things of this world to confound the strong. We see that theme in the Bible again and again. The world may say that something is insignificant and unimportant and of no account, but God says, "Ah, that is the man, the woman, the group, I am going to use to accomplish my eternal plan."

At this point, we see that God also has a terrific sense of humor. He will use the child of this inauspicious marriage to deliver a nation from Pharaoh, and who will train this deliverer? Pharaoh himself! I imagine God grinned every once in a while as he saw Pharaoh taking care of his adopted grandson, showing him how to pull a bow and how to drive a chariot. That is just like God; he doesn't waste anything. So if Pharaoh and all his minions know how to lead a great army, why not use them to train Moses?

I see something else intriguing in this account: the overabundant goodness of God. When the princess of Egypt looked at that baby boy, I don't think she could miss the fact that he was a Hebrew baby. But he was crying and her motherly heart reached out to him. Her servants put him in her arms, and just at that moment a little Hebrew girl appeared and said, "Ma'am, do you want me to find you a nurse for him?"

The princess answered, "Why, yes, he needs a nurse. Take him to a nurse and then bring him back to me, and I'll pay her."

So Jochebed, Moses' mother, cuddled her own little boy to her breast and the Pharaoh paid her out of his household budget! God didn't just give Jochebed's baby back to her; he gave her baby back with money. That is God's way, isn't it? To me, these little touches make the Bible all the more fascinating to read. It is just a little aside and yet so vivid, so alive, and so real. God speaks out of these details.

But something else in this second chapter is of as much importance as Moses' being pulled from the bulrushes, and that is Moses' killing a man. God is preparing the deliverer, right? So here he is: grown up fit and strong, with royal training and ability. More than that, he has compassion; he sees his people being oppressed and he wants to deliver them. So how is he going to do it?

He chooses to do it with human cunning. He murders a taskmaster on the sly and buries the evidence.

He chooses to do it with human strength. He was stronger than the slave's taskmaster—which was saying something, because those Egyptian taskmasters were big, tough, marine drill instructor types. But that was apparently no problem for Moses.

Moses seemed to think, *I am stronger than that fellow, so I will just smash him in my human strength and bury him in my human cunning. That's how I will deliver my people.*

But he failed, and I believe that failure was as important as anything else that occurred in Moses' life. Right here, we have the age-old conflict between trying to do right in the flesh—in our human wisdom, human ability, and human will—and trying to do right in the power of the Spirit, with divine wisdom, ability, and will. Who was going to deliver God's people? Moses thought he could do it. Yes, sir. But when his treachery was discovered, Moses crept out of Egypt in ignominy and despair, saying, "God, I can't do this. It is no good; it is over."

And I imagine God said, "I am glad you learned that."

You see, no lesson in life is as important as the lesson of, "I cannot." Why has God so often used the castoffs and leftovers of the human race to accomplish his will? Because strong, clever, confident people seldom learn that they cannot do it. The mighty, the powerful, the noble, and the great go through life thinking, *Ah, that was just a little setback. I can do it; I can handle it; I can make it.* They have not learned the lesson that they cannot do extraordinary things, not even with extraordinary human ability. They have never allowed the Spirit of God to be poured out upon them. So Moses' failure was as important to his preparation as anything else that happened. When he said, "I guess it's all over; I guess God's people are not going to be delivered," I think there was a smile on God's face. That broken man could now be filled with the Spirit of God so that when God's people were delivered, they would say, "Moses is a great man, but God delivered us. God did it."

Why is that important? Because only God can deliver us; any apparent deliverance by human might is a fraud. Any church built upon human wisdom, human skill, or human wealth is doomed to destruction. Any organization built on the flesh is as mortal as physical flesh, but any work done in the Spirit of God is as eternal as God himself.

God says to you and me, "You are just one, but that is all I need. I need you to be the person that I made you to be. I need you to be the one who will give me yourself in your failure, in your distress, and in your trouble. I need you to be the one who will say, 'Lord, I trust you. I believe that in this thing you will reveal yourself to me. Despite my weakness and inadequacy, I believe you will enable me by the power of your Spirit to do the thing for which I was made.'"

## Our Hope Is in God

Exodus 2:23–25 provides an important transition between the preparation of the deliverer and the call of the deliverer. After Moses the impulsive deliverer had failed, he fled to the land of Midian, which seems to have been on both the east and west sides of the Gulf of Elath, which separates the Sinai Peninsula from Arabia. There he married the daughter of a Midianite priest and she bore him a son. In verse 22, we are told that he named the child Gershom, which is Hebrew for "stranger," because he said, "I am a stranger in a foreign land." What a note of finality there is in this! The deliverer is living on the back side of the desert and he names his child "stranger" because, as far as Moses knows, that is all he will ever be for the rest of his life. But, thank God, our assessment of our situation is never the last word. So verse 23 says, "Now it happened in the process of time, that the king of Egypt died. Then the children of Israel groaned because of the bondage, and they cried out; and their cry came up to God because of their bondage" (NKJV). Our deliverance does not depend on the success or the failure of any human agent. Our deliverance depends only upon God, who hears our groaning. Scripture says, "And God looked on the children of Israel and God knew them." Aren't you glad to know we have such a God who can see our trouble, hear our cries, and identify himself with us? He knows our predicament. He does not say, "I don't know those slaves; I only know the successful people. I know the beautiful people, not those failing, broken, weak people. No, I have never seen them." Thank God that is not our God. He sees and he hears what is happening to us. Whatever you are going through, know that the God who hung the Big Dipper sees it all. He hears every mumbling, muttered groan from your lips. Every time I think about that, I get what teenagers call a "brain cramp." How many people do you suppose are praying right now in the world? A billion? Perhaps. But God hears each of those voices. He knows and cares about what each one is saying. The Lord says, "That's my girl, that's my boy. I know them." Thank God.

He also remembers the promises he has made to us. Exodus 2:24 says, "He remembered His covenant" (NKJV). Now these people had lived four hundred years in paganism, so it is highly unlikely that they remembered very much about God. Many of them undoubtedly were involved in pagan practices. How easily God could have said, "These people are not like Abraham, Isaac, or Jacob. They are a long, long way from their spiritual roots. I don't have any commitment to them. I don't have any bond to them. They don't have any claim on me." But no, that's not how God responded. God says, in effect, "I remember what I said to Abraham about his future, and his children, and his children's children, and his children's children's children. I remember my promise." God does not change with the changing of the seasons or geopolitical fortunes. He does not promise one thing today and forget it tomorrow; he is faithful to his promises.

# Questions for Personal Study or Discussion

1. What three things did God promise to Abraham, Sarah, and their family?

2. In what part of Egypt did the Hebrew slaves live? What problem did this pose to the Egyptians?

3. Exodus 1:17 describes two Hebrew midwives who "feared the Lord." What were a couple of ways they demonstrated this fear? What's the difference between a healthy fear of God and an unhealthy fear of him?

4. Dr. Oswalt says, "God's salvation is never by means of some broad, impersonal program; it is a personal transaction." Name a few people besides Moses that God has used to save his people from physical bondage or spiritual darkness.

5. Do you see evidence that you might be a significant part of God's eternal plan? Has anyone ever told you this?

6. After Moses murdered a man, he despaired that he would amount to anything until God spoke to him through the burning bush. Have you ever fallen into a similar mood of despair? Are you there now?

7. How has God spoken to you in a time of despair? What unusual circumstances might he be using to try to speak to you now?

# CHAPTER 3

# The Call of the Deliverer
## (Exodus 3:1–4:27)

The third part of God's preparation to deliver his people is the call of the deliverer. This is primarily found in Exodus 3–4. The deliverer's call grows directly out of the reality that we discussed at the end of the last chapter—i.e., the personal involvement of God with the Israelites and his awareness of their condition.

One thing I have discovered in my own life is that it is hard to get God to let go of you. When God lays his hand on you, it is difficult to get away. As I teach in seminary, I hear the life stories of so many students. Again and again, this is what I hear: Sometime in the student's childhood, that tender, childish heart opened up to God and the individual has never been able to get away from the reality of that moment. They may have backslidden; they have gone through the teenage troubles; they may have experienced heart-wrenching tragedies; but they can't get away from the love of God. That's how it was for the Hebrew people. Their deliverance from Egypt did not depend on whether Moses was so smart or so well-trained or shrewd. All of Moses' leadership qualities would be a part of it, of course, because God uses human agents. But their deliverance depended primarily on God. The Hebrew at prayer wondered aloud, "Does God know my condition? Does he care? Does he remember his promises to us? Is he going to keep them?" And the answer is, yes, yes, yes, and yes. That is God.

Because he knows, because he cares, because he remembers, he reaches out across the miles to a lonely, forgotten old man watching a bunch of sheep on "the back side of the desert." Moses has given up. He believes he's useless. He thinks his life is over. But no, it is not. God is never done with us until his purpose is fulfilled. God always has new possibilities for us wherever we are and whatever is happening.

## The Burning Bush

The opening event in the call of Moses is a strange experience narrated in Exodus 3:1–6. I've noticed this about the Bible: It will allow ten or twenty years to go by in a character's life and not tell us a thing about what happened; then it will devote two chapters to an incident that may have taken fifteen minutes. Why? I believe it is because those moments when God breaks in can change the direction of our lives forever. In those special moments, every detail is significant. Why did God choose this burning bush that was not consumed? Did he just say, "Ah, we need something to catch Moses' attention. What would be a good show-stopper?" I don't think so. Every detail of this narrative is significant. God could have revealed himself differently if he had wanted to; the fact that he did it this way means the details are important.

I believe the bush that burned but was not consumed is a parable of the flesh and the Spirit. When you try to serve God in your own strength, in your own ability, in your own wisdom, you will burn up. You will be consumed. You will be the fuel for that fire, and as long as there is fuel in you, there will be a fire.

But eventually your fuel will be exhausted, and then the fire will go out. That had happened to Moses: he had tried to deliver his people in his own strength, and that strength wasn't enough. So I think God is saying to Moses, "Look here, son. See something that radiates my light but is not the fuel for it. That is what I want you to be. I want you to show forth my light, but I am not going to burn you up because you're not the fuel. The oil of my Spirit can fuel the fire that burns in your life. Will you let me do that?"

This is the lesson of the bush that burns but is not consumed. It is what God was saying to Moses, and he is saying the same to you and me. Some of us are burned out. We have struggled, we have striven, we have served God with all we had, and we are spent. So we say, "I can't go on."

And God says, "I am glad to hear that. I wondered how long it would take you to get to this point. You are not the fuel, my child. You are the light bearer, but my Spirit is the fuel for the fire—if you will let him be."

The best thing you or I can say is, "Lord, I want to be used by you, but I am done. I've burned out." Only then can the Lord say, "Good, let's go." He said that to Moses in the bush that burned but was not consumed, and I believe it is the essence of life of the Spirit—to be a light for God yet not be consumed by the burning.

What a delight it is to see some people who are farther down the road of Christian life than we are! Their faces are like road maps—covered with blue lines and red lines, perhaps even some four-lane lines, but they are lines of joy, contentment, and peace. They are a witness to us. "Come on," they say, "the way is long, but our Guide is faithful. The Lord doesn't consume us. He doesn't destroy us. He is the light that shines through us." That is what I want for my life when I come to the end of the way, don't you?

Out of the fire, God says, "Moses, Moses," and Moses says in Hebrew, "Behold me." Those are the very same words that Abraham said back in Genesis 22 when God called him to sacrifice his son, Isaac. I suspect Isaac was just about the age of puberty and had not yet driven Abraham and Sarah crazy. I can imagine Abraham sitting there by the tent flap, looking at his only child and no doubt thinking that the sun rose and set on him. Then he hears, "Abraham."

"Behold me, Lord. I have nothing to hide from you. I know you love me. I know I can trust you. I know I can believe you. Here I am. What do you want?"

Oh, how different from the response of Adam, millennia before! "Adam?" God called (see Gen 3:8 ff.).

"You can't see me, I am behind this bush. Don't look at me. Don't look into my heart. Don't see what's here. I am afraid of you. You will kill me. You will destroy me."

What was Abraham's response?" "Behold me."

Moses' response? "Behold me."

Years later, when God said, "I wish there was somebody that I could send to my people," Isaiah was quick to answer, "Hey, God! Hey, here I am! Could you use me?" (see Isa 6:8).

How our fearful hearts betray us! Do we dare to let God get close? We think, *No, he'll burn me up. He will consume me. He will leave me a burned out, blackened ash. I won't let him do that. I won't answer.*

But Moses says, "Here I am." So God says, "Take your shoes off" (see Ex 3:5).

What? Why should Moses take his shoes off? God explains that the ground on which Moses is standing is holy. Why? Although the Bible does not make it specific, the answer is clear: The ground itself is holy because God is there.

People will sometimes say, "The ancient people were not like us moderns. We divide the sacred from the secular, but to the ancient people all the world was sacred." There is some truth to that statement, because pagans have generally believed the whole world is divine. But if that were true, the whole world would also be profane, because we see both clean and unclean, good and evil, in this world. Pagans ironically believe that since all of the world is sacred, none of it is sacred. No part of the world can cleanse any other part of the world because it is all equally filthy. Therefore, they call everything sacred.

No, the Bible says, certain places and times are sacred because God is particularly there—the God who exists apart from this world, the God who breaks into this world. When he shows up in our world, he cleanses it, renews it, and makes it holy with his presence. So he says, "Moses, I am here. I am the Other. I am the One beyond you; I am the One beyond the world. I am the One beyond the touch of human hands; I am the Other, and I am here, and that means this dirt is different from the dirt on the bottoms of your shoes. Take them off."

Thank God, there is One who is holy. Thank God, he is not this world. Thank God, he can break into this world and whatever he touches becomes like him. That is what he was saying to Moses in that moment: "Moses, I am not you. I am not Pharaoh. I am not Egypt. I am not the dirt or the sun or the moon or the stars. I am not your affections or your feelings. I am Other than anything you have ever experienced, and I have broken into your experience. I bring what is clean and true and pure and living. Will you embrace this? Then take your shoes off. Recognize the holy ground. Recognize that the Other has met here with you and speaks to you in this moment."

What follows? Look at verses 7–10 and notice the pronouns. They reveal what the narrator is trying to get across. Verse 7: "I have seen the oppression of my people...I know their sorrows." Verse eight: "So I have come down to deliver..." Verses 9–10: "The cry of the children of Israel has come to me, and I have also seen the oppression with which the Egyptians oppress them. Come now, therefore, and I will send you to Pharaoh that you may bring My people...out of Egypt" (NKJV). Eight times in four verses, a first-person pronoun (*I, my, me*) appears. Who is going to deliver the Hebrews? God is. If the Hebrew people ever get delivered, it will be an act of God. God makes that so plain right here at the outset of Moses' call. He does not say, "Now, Moses, I have chosen you because you have the ability and the desire to accomplish this task. You are a cunning man. Besides that, you are a Hebrew. So I need you to pull this off. I'm sure you can do it"

No, indeed! God says, "I have heard the cry of my people, and I will deliver my people. And I will bring my people out of Egypt, through you." That is the call of God. The call of God does not depend on the person being called; it depends on God. That is the central theme running through this whole passage. Is this call of God about Moses, or is it about God?

## The Objections

That question ("Is this about God, or is it about me?") is really at the heart of what follows in 3:11–4:17. Here Moses' raises four concerns that he thinks disqualify him for the commission that God wants to give him. All of them relate to deficits on Moses' side of the ledger. The first objection appears in 3:11—"Who am I? I am nobody. I am worse than a nobody. I am a criminal nobody in Egypt!" The second question appears in 3:13—"What shall I say? I don't even know your name." The third objection comes in 4:1—"They won't believe me. They'll say I have made up all of this." The final objection has a certain air of desperation about it (4:10)—"And anyway, I stutter." Did you notice the pronouns? Moses says, "The reason I can't go is because I am not adequate. I am nobody. I don't know what to say. I don't have the kind of charisma that makes people want to do what I say, and I can't even talk without stuttering. I am inadequate for this call."

### Who Am I? (3:11–12)

Now notice God's answers. Just as Jesus often did when replying to his questioners, God has a disconcerting way of answering another question that Moses was really asking, not what he had overtly asked. God says in response to Moses' first question, "I will be with you" (3:12). The issue is not who Moses is, just as the issue was not how good the bush was for burning. What kind of fire was burning in it? And what kind of fire would be burning in Moses? Moses' real question was not, "What are my qualifications?" but, "God, are you in this?" And God answered that question when he declared he would go with Moses.

I suppose if I were God, I might have said, "Moses, come on. I have spent eighty years preparing you. You have wonderful administrative and military abilities. You have gotten the best training the Egyptians could give you. You have come from a wonderful home, you have a mother of faith. Egyptian is your native language, and..." But God doesn't touch any of that, because it is not the issue. Thank God for good qualifications. He ought to have the best, brightest, sharpest tools he can get, but that is not what's really on Moses' mind. He wonders, "Will you take me there and drop me, God? Will you set me at the front of the column and abandon me? Will you make me the leader and burn me up?" So God says, "I will be with you."

### What Is My Message? (3:13–22)

Next, Moses says, "I don't even know your name. What do I have to say to these people if I don't even know who you are?" Once again, God answers much more than Moses' superficial question implied. God says, "My name is I AM." What's the meaning of this?

From the rest of the Old Testament, it is clear that God's personal name was contained in the four consonants *YHWH*. Scholars believe that the name was pronounced "Yahweh."[1] If that conclusion is correct, then the name would mean either "he is," or "he causes to be." God identifies himself by that name again in Exodus 6:2–9, which we will discuss a bit later. However, that is not what God says here.

Here he says his name is 'EHYEH, or "I AM." What is going on? Is God's name "HE IS" (third person) or is it I AM (first person)? In the ancient world, a name is much more than a label; it

---

1. Our understanding of this name has a complicated history. When the Hebrews first began to write their language, they only used consonants. This may be because they only used written texts to jog their memories. But after the destruction of the temple in AD 70. and the forced deportation of Jews from Judah following the failed revolt of Bar Kochba in AD 135, Jewish scholars became concerned that God's Word be pronounced the same by Jews all over the world. As a result they developed a system for adding vowel markings into the consonantal text. These markings were added somewhere between AD 500 and 850. However, a problem had developed concerning God's name: it had become customary not to say God's personal name whenever the consonants *YHWH* were encountered, but to say 'adonai, "Lord," instead. So when vowels were inserted into the consonantal text, it was the vowels of 'adonai, –a–o–a–, which were inserted into the divine name, resulting in *yahowah*. Luther and his compatriots who made the German translation of the Hebrew Bible in the 1500s did not know what had happened and so transliterated what they thought to be the divine name as "Jehovah" (*j* standing for *y*, and *v* for *w* in German script). In fact, no such name existed in Old Testament times, and we are now forced to reconstruct the probable pronunciation based on the evidence of personal names incorporating the divine name and other similar kinds of evidence.

expresses one's nature and character. So when we read in Psalms that "God's name is glorious," that is not a statement about God's label but about his nature and character. So when God identifies himself as *Yahweh*, he is talking very explicitly about his nature. Moses is not going to be about giving his people some privileged information about God's identity. Rather, what he is going to say and demonstrate to them will reveal the very nature of the Godhead—that is, what the name means.

So what does *Yahweh* mean, and why does God change from third person to first person in this conversation to convey that meaning? Surely, it implies that Yahweh intends to have a first-person relationship with each of us. We do not have to speak about him in the third person, as someone we have heard or read about. We can speak to him in the first person. Yahweh wants to be on a first-name basis with his people. But what else does he mean when he refers to himself as the I AM? At the very least, it means that God is not locked into the past. The Hebrews knew that he was the God of Abraham, Isaac, and Jacob; but those patriarchs lived in the past, and they now confronted a new set of problems. If the work of God was limited to the past, he might not be able to help them escape from Egypt.

But Yahweh is not the "I WAS"; he is the "I AM." He was adequate for times past, certainly—he helped our grandmothers, our grandfathers, our fathers and mothers—but he is adequate for our days too. He was adequate for a situation that Abraham hardly even dreamed of when he looked up into the sky centuries before, and he was adequate for Moses' new situation.

But do you know something else? The I AM is also the God of the future. Notice what he does in verses 16–22. He tells the future. Only the God who stands outside of time and space, who is the eternal "I AM," can do that.

Isaiah makes this point again and again in chapters 40–46 of his book. Isaiah says that Yahweh had told his people about the exile and the return 150 years in advance. Pagan idols cannot do that because they are part of this world. They are wood and stone, subject to the laws of physics that prevail in the present world; they do not know the future, because they have no future. Pagans believe that what happened yesterday will happen again tomorrow; the cosmic story is an endless cycle. But the I AM is not caught in an endless cycle. He knows our tomorrows, knows what they will be like, and can tell us as much as we need to know in advance so that when it happens, we will not be taken off-guard.

So he tells Moses, "I know that Pharaoh won't let you go just because you swagger in there and say, 'Hello, Pharaoh, we are ready to leave.' He is not going to do it. He is going to harden his heart. But when you go...."

"Oh," Moses might have said, "you mean we are still going to leave Egypt, even if Pharaoh hardens his heart?"

"Yes, and when you go, you are going to take the wealth of Egypt with you."

"Why is that, God?"

But God does not tell him. We know the answer because we know the rest of the story. They would take the wealth of Egypt with them to build a glorious place for worshiping Yahweh in the middle of the camp. God was not ready to reveal that to Moses yet, but he disclosed enough to convince Moses that he was the God of the future.

We might paraphrase it this way: "I am the I AM. I am not the I WAS and not the I WILL BE, but in every time and place and circumstance, I AM God. I am adequate for everything that has happened, does happen, or will happen. I AM."

What else is Yahweh saying about himself when he introduces himself to Moses as I AM? He is saying that he is totally self-existent. He is dependent on nothing and no one else. Only one being in the universe can say that, because every other being is dependent on that one. Have you ever met a self-made man? That's a joke, isn't it? There is no such thing; every one of us is dependent on the world around us for our life. Suppose the building where you sit could be sealed hermetically and all the air pumped out. How long would you be able to say, "I am?" Not more than ten minutes. We are totally dependent upon on the mix of oxygen in the atmosphere around us for our lives. Suppose your water supply was shut off and you couldn't get any. How long could we say, "I am?" About eight days. Suppose all food was denied to you, how long would you last? Hunger strikers have shown us that fifty-five days is about the maximum. Are we really independent? Are we self-made individuals? Far from it!

But praise God, there is One who can say in all truth, "I AM." Though the stars go out, though the worlds die, though the sun explodes in a million fragments, God was, is, and will be. And the good news is that the I AM says to you and me, "I want to share my glory with you. I want you to live in my radiance, I want you to share my character, my nature, even my name. I AM." What a name that is!

Soldiers came creeping through a garden in the small hours of the morning. "Do you see him? Where is he? Be careful. Remember what he did to that herd of pigs."

Suddenly, a man stepped out from behind an olive tree and said, "What do you fellows want?"

"SHHHH," they said. "We are looking for Jesus of Nazareth." He responded, "I am."

Do you know what John says they did? They fell backwards on the ground (John 18:6). Of course they did; they knew what he had just said. The only way they could take I AM captive was if he freely surrendered himself to them, which is what he did, for us.

Those two words had echoed again and again throughout the ministry of this strange young man from Nazareth. One day, a mocking crowd cried out, "Our Father is Abraham. Who is your Father?" Jesus replied, "Before Abraham was, I AM." Those Jews knew exactly what he was saying, and they took up stones to stone him (John 8:32–58). No human dare call himself that because it is true only of God. Yet Jesus did.

Jesus is the I AM who has come into our time and space to show us the face of God. So when we say with Moses, "Others will want to know who you are. What is your name?" Jesus answers, "I AM. I AM." He is adequate for the past, the present, the future. He is the One who gathers all of existence into himself, the One who reaches out with nail-pierced hands to share that existence with us.

### What If They Reject Me? (4:1–9)

You'd think Moses would begin to get the picture, but he was persistent. So we come to his third objection in 4:1: "Suppose they reject me." In some ways, the need for acceptance is the strongest of all psychological needs. Rejection hurts when people hate us, but it hurts even more when they ignore us, when they act as if we did not exist. Who can bear that? So Moses says, "God, if the priests of Egypt pay no attention to me, what am I going to do? When I face the concentrated demonic powers of their old, settled idolatry, I am no magician, I am no sorcerer."

As in the first two instances, God does not try to bolster Moses' ego. He does not give Moses a pep talk to convince him that he will be quite persuasive after all. Remember, this is not about Moses; it is about the power of God and whether God can be trusted to be adequate for every circumstance. So God shows Moses how he will reveal his power to the magicians of Egypt, using two significant symbols: a snake and leprosy. They are significant because both are symbols of evil in the Old Testament. God was saying to Moses, "I give you power over evil. I give you power. You need not fear whatever may come against you. You need not fear whatever the world may throw at you. You need not fear whatever Satan may throw at you. Because I am with you, you will have the power to confront evil and triumph over it." Note that God did not grant Moses supernatural power to do mighty works whenever he chose; rather, God demonstrated that his divine hand would enable Moses to convince anyone who doubted him.

It is also significant to note that God did not choose some weird ritual or shamanistic mumbo-jumbo to prove that Moses was his emissary. God simply asked what was in Moses' hand, and Moses replied that it was his shepherd's rod—an everyday article and the sign of Moses' profession. "Throw it down," said Yahweh. When he did, the shepherd's rod became a snake. Then God commanded Moses to grab that snake by the tail (which is most definitely not the way to pick up a snake), and it immediately became a rod again.

I do not believe I am reading too much into this passage to say that the rod in your hand, whatever it is, will be useless as long as you insist on keeping it. The ordinary "rod" on which you depend may be a friend, a spouse, a home, a job, or even a hobby. Whatever it is, that rod is useless as long as you lean upon it, so God commands you to throw it down at his feet. If you do, he may not give it back. That is his business. But if he does give it back, he will transform that familiar thing into an instrument of his glory.

But God gives Moses a second sign. Now it is not what is in Moses' hand, but the hand itself. At God's command, Moses puts his hand inside his tunic. When he pulls it out, it is leprous. (Did Moses then say, "I'm sorry, God, but I can't go to Egypt: I am a leper"? If he did, God paid no attention.) God instructed him to thrust his hand inside his tunic again and take it out. His hand came out whole, with flesh as soft as a baby's.

Once again, it seems to me that the symbolism is very clear. Whatever we touch in our own strength, we will defile because there is no moral cleanliness in us. But God can cleanse that defilement. He can use our gifts and abilities to bless the world. So God says, "I will use you, Moses, and you will be clean. What you do for me and for them will not be defiled with your own self-serving."

God's presence, "I will be with you,"—that is what matters. God's person, I AM—that is what matters. God's power, "I will enable you to face whatever you need to face"—that is what matters. Moses is running out of objections; every one of them has come up against God's character and nature. Moses has tried to beg off due to his deficiencies, but God has said, "This assignment doesn't depend on you, Moses, it depends on me. It is not your identity, it is not your power, it is not your presence, it is not your intelligence that will free my people—it is mine. Do you know I will be with you? Do you know that I am who I am? Do you know that I have all power? That is the issue."

### I Cannot Talk (4:10–17)

But Moses marshals one more objection: "God, I'm sorry to tell you this, but I can't talk." From God's response, it appears that he is getting a bit exasperated. "Who made man's mouth, Moses? Who makes the deaf, the seeing, or the blind? Have not

I, the Lord? For heaven's sake, Moses, I made your mouth. Now go, and I will be with your mouth. I will teach you what to say."

Moses now is at rock bottom. It took God a while to get him there, but he finally did. "O Lord," Moses says, "please send someone else to do it" (Ex 4:13). Here it is. Moses simply does not want to do what God commands him to do.

You know, this is the critical question for every one of us. When we hesitate to answer God's call, the question is not really about our excuses, our explanations, or all the other stuff. The question is, Will you or will you not obey God?

Now God is more than exasperated with Moses; he is angry. But he is not finished with Moses. In his marvelous creativity, he says, "Is not Aaron the Levite your brother? I know he can speak well. Look, he is coming to meet you. When he sees you, he will be glad in his heart." Perhaps Moses thought, *Well, I won't be glad. You set me up for this, God. You had this all prepared. You had Aaron on the road three days ago, knowing I would backpedal like this. You knew what I would do. You knew what I am like.*

Do you see God grinning a little?

What follows is remarkable. Look at 4:18: "So Moses went and returned to Jethro his father-in-law and said to him, 'Please let me go and return to my brethren who are in Egypt.'"

The Bible says not a word about a moment when Moses' heart melted and he said, "OK, God, you win. I am going to obey you." There's no description of how lightning flashed, thunder roared, and Moses jumped up and down with joy, shouting, "Isn't it good to serve God?" Not a word. Not a word.

Perhaps there was such a moment and it was too precious for us to peer into. There are moments that are not supposed to be shared. Perhaps in final surrender to the love embrace of God, Moses and God just enjoyed each other for a while.

But suppose there was not such an emotional breakthrough moment. Suppose Moses simply said, "I have no more excuses. I am either going to do God's will or I am not going to do his will. I know what his will is, and I must not disobey him, so I am going to do it." Sometimes that is the way it is. Sometimes God doesn't give us any confirmation of our obedience for days or months or even years. Nevertheless, the pivotal question is whether we are we going to obey him. It doesn't matter whether we have a great emotional catharsis when we do. As soon as we know what God expects of us, we must do it.

I do not want to oversimplify the business of discerning God's will. Sometimes we preachers make that appear a lot simpler than it is. The truth is, it may take days, months, even years for us to be sure what God wants of us. But when, in my heart of hearts, I know what God's will is, then without another word I am going to do it. Thank God, in the moment when Moses knew—when the glory and the power, the providence and the person of God were made perfectly clear to him—he told his father-in-law, "I must go to Egypt."

So chapters 3–4 record a divine moment in Moses' life. How long did it take? It doesn't take ten minutes to read about it, and I suspect it probably did not take much longer than that, in fact. But however long it took, the future of the world hung on that moment. I am in no position to suggest that your divine moments are that critical, but perhaps they are. Be ready for them.

## The Incident on the Road (4:24–26)

After this great climax, we come upon one of the strangest incidents in the entire Bible. Moses is on the road to Egypt. He has accepted Yahweh's call, has taken his leave from father-in-law

Jethro, and is on his way to confront the Pharaoh. He is obeying God, yet God tries to kill him (Ex 4:24)! What is going on here?

The account is so brief and so mysterious that any interpretation must necessarily be very tentative. However, here is one possibility. Moses was going back to Egypt to announce that God is faithful. Who is this God? He is the God who made a covenant with Abraham, committing himself to the patriarch. He is the same God who now is going to keep faith with Abraham's descendants. But not only was Moses going to announce that the Abrahamic Covenant was still true, he was going to announce a further covenant in which Yahweh would reveal more of himself to his people and call them to give themselves to him on a much deeper level than Abraham had. Moses' was ultimately called to announce to Abraham's descendants, "Here is the Covenant God. He is faithful, and he calls you to be faithful. You can believe in him and enter into covenant with him." And yet Moses had not thought enough of the covenant to circumcise his own son.

What was so important about circumcision? Moses himself would say later that "circumcision of the heart" was what really mattered (Deut 10:16), yet physical male circumcision was an outward symbol of having surrendered yourself to God. Across the ancient Near East, the erect male penis was a symbol of power, of one's ability to dominate and reproduce oneself. It is not accidental that it was after the incident of Ishmael (Gen 16), in which Abraham tried to use his own reproductive power to keep God's promise for him, that Yahweh called on Abraham to prove his submission to God in the covenant act of circumcision (Gen. 17:10–11). To be sure, the problem with humanity is not the male genitalia; it is with our stubborn will, our "stony" hearts (Ezek 36:26). Yet male circumcision was an outward sign of a people's inward submission. Their refusal to accept this sign was a symptom of a much deeper problem.

It is very easy in the midst of an exciting, moving, convicting time to make a lot of fervent professions of obedience to God. In a time of great religious passion, it's easy to say, "O Lord, I love you so much I will do anything for you!" And we will do everything except the simple, obvious, commanded obedience that God requires of us. For instance, there is his command to make one day out of seven different from all the rest—some very obvious, simple things like that. On the other hand, we may seem perplexed about the will of God. "O God, what do you want me to do?" we cry out. (I wonder if God does not say, "I have told you, over and over and over again; start there with my commandments.")

At any rate, Moses was going to Egypt to proclaim the covenant of God, even though he did not think enough of that covenant to obey even its smallest command. And God seems to say, "If you are going with that attitude, you would be better off dead."

Today, it is very easy for us to take God for granted. It is very easy to act as though God were a benign little being who exists to help us out of our troubles. But he is the almighty God, in whom is all the power and holiness of the universe. Yet we fool around with him as if he were unimportant and insignificant. God could well say, "Children, be careful. If you treat me as though I do not matter, I am dangerous."

Imagine you are walking through an electric substation. There is an ominous humming in the wires because so much electric power is coursing through them. How are you going to proceed through there? Are you going to skip and dance, flippantly touching everything you see? I suspect not; I suspect that you would walk very deliberately and carefully. Why? Do you think electricity hates you? Do you think you cannot trust it? No, but your nature and the nature of electricity are so different that if they come into casual contact, you are in serious trouble. That is how it is with us and God. God does not want to destroy us any more than electricity does. But here the analogy comes to its limits, because God is no impersonal, inanimate force. He loves us and wants to bless us. But we must imagine him saying, "You can't fool around with me. You can't treat me as a little idol that you carry around for your benefit. I am God."

Now I am convinced that Moses and Zipporah had discussed the matter of circumcision beforehand. Why? Because the instant Moses got sick or whatever it was that happened to him, Zipporah grabbed a knife and circumcised their child in nothing flat. She knew immediately what the trouble was. Isn't it fascinating that a foreign convert was more sensitive to the will of God at that moment than her believing husband was? Perhaps that was why she hurled the piece of flesh at Moses' feet, as if to say, "If you are going to serve God, you had better serve him with all you have."

If you are going to serve God, you had better serve him with your whole heart. If you are going to serve God, you had better resolve at the beginning that you are going to obey the whole will of God. It is not because he is a mean, evil person who is trying to hold you to every line and dot. No, perfect obedience is important because, given God's incredible holiness, we will get ourselves killed if we come into his presence with a casual, uncaring attitude. So Yahweh's confrontation with Moses was his way of saying, "If you are going to go and proclaim my covenant, then you'd better conform to that covenant yourself."

## Questions for Personal Study or Discussion

1.  What do you think is the most peculiar aspect of Moses' burning bush experience? Why?

2.  Dr. Oswalt sees a parallel between God's call to Moses and his call to two of Moses' ancestors. Who were they? How were their responses different?

3.  Why did Moses have to take his shoes off to approach the burning bush? How do we convey this same idea in our church buildings? Our worship services? How do we convey it in our lives?

4.  What are some differences between God and manmade idols that are emphasized by his name (I AM)?

5.  Is any part of God's message through the burning bush troubling to you as you think about your own relationship with God? Does anything about the bush message reassure you?

6.  Describe in your own words what you think Moses meant by "circumcision of the heart"(Deut 10:16).

7.  Is anything so distinctive about your life as a believer that the world would see it as a kind of circumcision? If so, does that attract other people to you or alienate them from you?

# CHAPTER 4

# The Offer of Deliverance
## (4:27–6:30)

## Hardening of Pharaoh's Heart

As Moses and his family started down the road to Egypt, Yahweh said something to Moses that must have been a little chilling. God might have said, "Now I am going to go before you and prepare the way. Pharaoh will see the light right away and you will leave Egypt with no problems." But God said the very opposite: "I will harden his heart, so that he will not let the people go" (4:21 NKJV). What is going on here, anyway? Is a gracious, merciful God making it impossible for Pharaoh to repent? Well, that is what many people believe, and in just looking at the statement, you can see why they might think that. Not only does God say it here; he says it again in 7:3 and in 9:12.

But look closely at 3:19: "I know that *he* will harden his heart." Oh, Pharaoh has got something to do with it as well? Now look at 7:13: "His heart *became* hard." These verses indicate that the hardening would take place, not because God would arbitrarily do it against Pharaoh's own will, but because God foreknew the process. This is said again in 7:22 and 8:19. Then most significantly, in 8:15 we read, "He hardened his heart." That is, as 3:19 predicted: Pharaoh hardened his own heart.

So we do not have in Exodus a picture of a good, kindly, reasonable monarch who is predisposed to treat the Israelites justly until he hears God say, "No, you can't!" Rather, we encounter here a proud, powerful, dominating individual who considers himself to be a god. Softening his heart and letting his valuable slaves go—especially at the command of some foreign god he does not even recognize—is the farthest thing from his consciousness. Whatever else we say, this much is clear: God is not doing something to Pharaoh against his will. No, whatever God does is entirely in keeping with Pharaoh's will. Pharaoh, exercising his own will, would never let those people go, not for an instant. He intended to get full value for his money out of them. He was using them for his construction projects. He was using them to realize his vision for domination. There was no way in which Pharaoh would choose to let those people go. So why does God send Moses on this errand, only to predict that he will fail?

I think two things are implied by this statement. First, God's world is so made that our choices are more and more predetermined by the choices we have already made. God's world makes it relatively easy to continue traveling on the life road we have chosen. The second thing God is saying in this warning to Moses is that Pharaoh is not a god. The only absolutely free being in the universe is God himself, the "I AM." Pharaoh thought that since he was a god, he was absolutely free to do as he pleased. But that was a fatal error. His choices, like all of ours, were constrained by the plans, purposes, and standards that the one Creator God has built into his creation.

Let's think more carefully about the first point. Is it really true that choosing one way makes us all the more likely to choose it again the next time we have a choice? Is the world really made that way? Yes, it is. Jesus' disciples asked him, "Why do you talk in parables?" His answer was, "So that those who don't want to understand, can't" (Matt 13:10–14). "But wait," you may say, "I thought Jesus spoke in parables so the truth would be crystal-clear to everybody." No, his parables only made his teaching crystal-clear to those who wanted to believe. But those who did not want to believe shook their heads and muttered to one another, "There he goes again, telling those strange little stories. Do you have any idea what he is talking about?"

"No, he's just a homespun storyteller from Galilee, that's all."

In other words, God has so made the world so that the choices you and I make tend to lead us to other choices in that same direction. This does not mean that we are locked into our present course of action forever; God does not give up on us simply because we have made some bad choices. He keeps on giving us opportunities to believe. That is what every one of those Egyptian plagues would be: another opportunity for Pharaoh to believe. But every time that Pharaoh said, "No," it became that much easier for him to defy God the next time, and the next, and the next. Given who Pharaoh was, who he thought himself to be, what he was determined to have, and the way God made us, it would become less and less likely that Pharaoh would turn against his own way.

What about the second point? Remember that at its heart, this whole series of events was a contest between God and the gods (12:12). The underlying question was, "What (or who) is the ultimate cause of all things?" The world in which these people were living, Egyptians and Israelites alike, imagined that there were thousands of gods. As a result, most people believed it was virtually impossible to know why anything happened. Perhaps a toothache god gave me a toothache this morning, or a stomachache goddess gave me a stomachache. (Never mind the green apples I ate yesterday.) Who knew why anything happened? But the Hebrew religion said everything that happens can be traced back to one single Cause: Yahweh, the Creator God. Everything that happens can be understood as being in line with his purposes or not in line with them. Even Pharaoh might not be able to recognize why he so stubbornly refused to let his precious slaves escape, but ultimately it had to do with one thing: his relationship to Yahweh. Nothing happens in our lives apart from our relationship to him.

We should note that this is not the kind of determinism that characterizes Islam, in which everything that happens is directly caused by Allah. God does not determine every choice we make or orchestrate every event that occurs in our lives. If I get a broken arm because my ax slips and my arm hits the tree, it is not because God says, "Oswalt is getting a little cocky, so I think I'll bring him down a bit. I'll make that ax slip." Never! But everything that happens in our lives can be traced back through a chain of causes to God, the way that he has designed the world and what he has permitted it to become. So if I am ill, it is not a surprise to God. If I am in trouble, it does not take God off guard. And because it does not, he is able to work in and through these things to accomplish his good purposes.

In other words, the Bible is saying in Exodus 4 and 5, "Do not think that Pharaoh is some independent god who can decide, 'I will or I won't,' without any reference to the Creator of the universe. Ultimately, every choice Pharaoh makes is within God's purposes and plans, so God sees them in advance."

We must keep those two factors, human choice and divine purpose, clearly in mind because both will determine the outcome of Moses' mission. On the one hand, Pharaoh has a will which he is free to exercise. On the other hand, none of his choices are made outside of the larger purposes and plans of God. God does not simply watch the world make its decisions, all the time figuring out how he is going to react to them.[1] And yet we dare not say that God is some sort of cosmic puppet master, who pulls our strings and makes us act out his little morality play. God does not arbitrarily decide who is saved and who is lost, for his own selfish glory. The truth lies between those extremes. Every human being has a will and an array of life-critical choices to make, but none of those choices are made outside of the overarching providences and purposes of God.

## Meeting with Aaron (4:27–28)

So Moses and Zipporah traveled on, and, sure enough, here came Aaron on the way to meet them. So Moses went and kissed him. Why do you suppose they did that? Was it simply a desert custom? No, I think it was because they each realized the faithfulness of God in meeting the other. Aaron was coming at the command of God, all the while wondering, *What will old Moses be like when I meet him? Is he going to think I am a fool when I say that God told me to be his mouthpiece?* And I believe Moses was wondering, *Will Aaron really come? I felt God say he was on the road, but I wonder if that was all just my imagination?* Then around the curve of the road comes Aaron. They run to each other, embrace, and kiss each other, not only because they had been separated for many years, but also because they each see in the other a confirmation of the faithfulness of God.

Yes, God is dependable, so we know we can commit our lives to him. Those experiences are priceless when we dare to believe him, step out tentatively in faith, and then something happens

---

1. We Arminians are in danger here if we assume that everything is up to us humans. God makes decisions too, and God can act to change our circumstances.

that confirms, Yes, this is of God. What a joy! What an experience of faith rewarded!

So Moses and Aaron went on toward Egypt, full of excitement and anticipation. God had called, God had promised, and God had fulfilled his promise. Surely the future was bright.

## The Initial Offer (4:29–31)

We come now to the offer of deliverance. Moses and Aaron told their people everything that God had said. They performed all the miracles and signs that God had given them to perform. And what was the result? The people believed! Well, why wouldn't they? God had clearly appeared to Moses and through him to Aaron, and what they said on God's behalf was wonderful. No more slavery. No more trouble. No more pain. No more oppression. God had noticed what they were going through and was going to take action. Of course "they bowed their heads and worshiped" (Ex 4:31 NKJV) in gratitude and faith. Why not?

If you have been involved in Christian work very long, this will sound very familiar. We say to people, "You have a problem with guilt and fear and need. Well, we have good news for you. Jesus gave his life for you. He has come to earth as the Divine Son of God to take away your sins and your guilt. He has come to solve the problems that are the result of your rebellion against the righteousness of God. Jesus has come to deliver you." In response, people say, "Yes, that is good news! I'll have some of that. If Jesus will solve all my problems, if Jesus will deliver me out of my sins, if Jesus will save me from my troubles, I want Jesus."

There is only one thing wrong with this way of sharing the gospel. It suggests that people should accept Jesus so that they will not have any more problems. But the truth is, for most of us, accepting Jesus is just the beginning of trouble.

Certainly, if you accept Jesus, you may have a great sense of peace and relief and deliverance. If you accept Jesus, you may have a new purpose, a new direction, and a new glory in your life. I do not deny any of that. But so long as you are living for the devil, you are no threat to him and his plans. As soon as you declare that you have switched sides—as soon as you say, "I am not going to live for you anymore, Satan. I am going to live for Jesus"—you raise your head up out of the trenches. And soldiers who raise their heads will be targeted. If we say to people, "Accept Jesus because you won't have any more problems," we do them a grave disservice. They ought to accept Jesus because there is no other way to live. They ought to accept Jesus because there is no other way to abundant, eternal life. They ought to accept Jesus because the Son of God gave his life for us. Troubles will come and go, but we should accept Jesus because there is no other way to live. So it has always been for people who declare themselves for God.

## Opposition (5:1–21)

Indeed, this is what took place for the Hebrews. Exodus 5 describes the trouble that arose when Israel accepted God's initial offer of deliverance, and the opposition that unfolds in chapter 6 reveals their real problem. As I said at the outset, physical oppression was a grave problem for the Hebrews, but it was not their deepest problem. The root problem of the Hebrews was that they did not know God. Unless they came to know him, deliverance from Egypt would only be a Band-Aid to their fatal wounds and not real healing.

In this way, troubles can bring us great spiritual blessings. How? It can happen if the trouble teaches us who we are, who God is, and who we really need. That's what was going on here. Why didn't God just work some climatic miracle? Why didn't he pick them up, carry them across the Sinai, and drop them in Canaan? That is what he wanted to do; he wanted to deliver them from bondage. He wanted to bring them into the land of promise. So why did he not just do it? Because if he had transported them from Egypt to Canaan without their ever really understanding who he was, he would not have saved them. He would have left them in spiritual bondage. If God were to take you out of your troubles today and suddenly make you rich, famous, comfortable, and prosperous, without your really knowing God, that would not be blessing. The greatest blessing is to know who God is and to know him personally as the Lord of your life.

So here God was saying, "No, I am not just going to take you to the Promised Land. I am going to bring both you and the Egyptians to know who I am."

We see this at the very outset of chapter five. Moses came into that glowing golden throne room to stand before the one whom the Egyptians took to be a god incarnate and said, "Yahweh says, 'Let my people go.'"

I suppose Pharaoh's jaw dropped. "Who is the Lord [Yahweh], that I should obey him and let Israel go? I do not know the Lord" (Ex 5:2). There it is. Pharaoh did not know who Yahweh was.

Pharaoh spoke the fundamental question of the whole human race: "Who is the Lord, that I should obey him? Look, I am the god of my life. I make my own decisions. I choose what, when, where, and how. Who is this Yahweh that I should obey him?"

That is a good question. Who is God anyway? Who is the Source of all being? Who is the sole Creator of the Universe?

Who could say "I AM" before the whole cosmos came into being? Answer that question and all of the other answers you need will flow from it. You will have found the way. You will have found life. So this is the essential human question: Who is the Lord, that I should obey him?

Moses and Aaron told him (5:3), and God was right: Pharaoh hardened his heart and said he didn't know any Yahweh, so he was not going to obey him. "Get back to your work!" he declared (5:4).

Pharaoh's thought processes here are very interesting. They go something like this:

1. I am god, because I don't know of anyone superior to me,
2. so Moses and Aaron could not have been told by another god to demand that I release my slaves.
3. Therefore, there must be some other explanation for where they got this terrible idea.

Once you reject the truth about anything, you must construct a false explanation for it. That is what happened here. Pharaoh concluded that the Hebrews had too much time on their hands because they were thinking up crazy things about imaginary gods, so he resolved to work them harder. (We see the same dynamic at work in American society today. We are constructing false answers as fast as we can because we refuse to believe the truth about our situation.)

If you attended Sunday school as a child, you remember the Egyptian brick story. To get a mud brick to hold together while it is drying in the sun, or in some cases while it is being fired in a kiln, brick makers must put some sort of binder material in it. Sometimes they use sea shells. In Egypt, they used stubble. So the Hebrew slaves put stubble in the mud to make the brick hold its shape while it was drying. Until Moses and Aaron arrived on the scene, the Egyptians had been giving the Hebrews stubble to use in the brick-making. But now, at Pharaoh's direction, they began to say, "Go collect your own stubble, but don't make any fewer bricks." Double the workload; that would keep their minds off this stupid business of serving some unknown god.

We often do the same sort of thing: God begins to deal with us—to point out an area in our lives that is displeasing to him or direct us in a new way—and we do not like it any more than Pharaoh did. So what do we do? We work harder. We throw ourselves into redoubled activity so that we won't have time to listen to the voice of God. That is exactly what Pharaoh thought he could do. If he could get the Hebrews so busy that they did not have any discretionary time, he would not have to worry about this silly Yahweh talk any more.

That strategy was useless then and it is useless now. God has a way of "coming in through the plumbing," you might say. No one can work hard enough to get away from him.

However, the slaves' work did get harder and harder. The Hebrews began to grumble and they failed to meet their daily quotas. So the Egyptian taskmasters began to bear down on the Hebrew foremen, saying, "Come on, get your people working faster; make them produce more." The upshot was that the Hebrew foremen went to Pharaoh and complained, "There is no straw given to your servants, and they say to us, 'Make bricks.' Indeed your servants are beaten, but the fault is in your own people, Pharaoh." And he said, "You are idle. That is why you say, 'Let's go and sacrifice to the Lord'" (5:15–19).

So the foremen left Pharaoh's audience chamber in a very foul mood. And who did they see coming in the door but Aaron and Moses? Somebody was going to get an earful. Most Bible translations try to avoid crude language, so the New International Version has the foremen say coolly, "May the Lord look on you and judge you" (5:21) But in fact, the best translation of what the foremen said is, "God damn you, Moses." And they were not using idle profanity; they really wanted that to happen.

## Deliverance: Issues Clarified (5:22–6:30)

How the foremen's response must have turned a knife in Moses' and Aaron's hearts! They had come to deliver God's people, and now God's people are saying, "God damn you. God judge you. God destroy you. Look what you have done to us. You come here with all your talk about God delivering us and solving our problems, but our problems are twice as bad today as before you came." So Moses went back to the Lord and questioned God's motives (5:22–23): "Why did you send me really?" Perhaps you have done something like that. At one time or another, you may have prayed, "I know what you said, God, but really, why did you put me in this situation? Did you do it so I would fail?"

But Moses went farther. He questioned not only Yahweh's motives but his character: "Lord, why have you brought evil on this people? Oh God, are you really good?" Have you ever asked questions like these? I have.

At Asbury Seminary we had a young man who was perhaps the brightest student on campus. He was certainly the brightest foreign student to come our way in a long time. He had been hand-picked by his denomination in Japan to come to this country and study to be their bright hope in the days to come. Then he was killed in a senseless automobile accident. "God, are you really good?" I asked. "Why didn't you snuff out the life of some drug pusher? Why him?"

You see what is happening in this section of the book of Exodus. The central question is coming into focus. That question is: Who is God? What can you believe about God in the dark times of life, when your hopes are crushed and you cannot see tomorrow? Who is God then? That is the real issue. You are well aware of your troubles, difficulties, and hardships; you are probably even aware of how you come to be in such a spot. But you wonder, *Is there a God who can work through these things and bring out of them light and hope?*

## Yahweh's Response (6:1–8)

Yahweh responds to that question in one of the most beautiful passages of Scripture. His offer of deliverance had made the Hebrews' problem worse. They had responded in fervent faith. They had all "come to the altar," as it were. But then they went back home and the world had fallen in on them. Why? Could God not be trusted? Did he not really want to do good for them? Or did he lack the power to do so? So God says to Moses, "Now you will see who I am. Now I have your attention, so you will see the full glory of my promises to you" (see 6:1). This issue haunts me. Are we ready to hear and see the promises of God? This is one reason for regular Bible study, exposing ourselves to the promises of God and hearing him say again and again, "You are mine. I will keep you. I will hold you." Fundamental to the validity of that promise is his identity. So he says in 6:2, "I am Yahweh, the Source of everything."

Our experience of the world hinges on whether we know that. Who is the Source of everything? You yourself? Your desires? Your plans? The inchoate forces of nature? Who is your god? There is only one God, Yahweh, and he has broken into time and space to reveal himself in the context of human historical experience.

So in Exodus 6, Yahweh describes himself by rehearsing what he has done in human history. He says, "This is who I am. I am the God who appeared to Abraham and Isaac and Jacob. I am the God who committed myself to them in covenant." That is a remarkable statement. In the pagan world, gods never committed themselves to anything. They wanted their worshipers to commit everything to them, but they made no promises on their own initiative. But right at the outset of the Scripture narrative, back in Genesis 12, this One who is the Source of everything, this One who needs nothing, this One who has absolute power, said, "I commit myself to bless you. I give myself to you and your descendants, Abraham. I give you these gifts that you long for." What kind of a god is this, who gives himself away without any strings attached?

That is the wonder of the cross. That is what Paul is talking about in Romans 5:8. God demonstrates, offers, "commends" his love toward us in that, while we were yet sinners, he gave his Son for us. That is our God, who commits himself to us without any prior obligation on our part.

So God said, "Moses, you are going to know that my character is to commit myself to human beings, as I have done to Abraham and Isaac." Then he said again that he had "heard and remembered" his people (see 2:24). In other words, God was saying, "I have a purpose in history. I said something back there, I committed myself, and I have never forgotten it. You can depend on me from the past into the present, and from the present into the future. I am that kind of God."

You and I may tend to yawn at that point. "Well, sure. Of course God is like that." Not necessarily. The pagans don't believe that. For the pagans, there is no past and no future, only the present moment. To their way of thinking, what has happened in the past has no bearing on what is about to happen.

I believe this is another symptom of America's slide into paganism. We believe all that matters is now. Give me pleasure—now. Give me satisfaction—now. Give me fullness of achievement—now. I don't care about anything else. But God says, "That is not the way I made the world. Your choices have consequences that affect the present and the future, and my promises can be trusted today and tomorrow and forever."

Yahweh says, "I made these promises to your forefathers, Moses. I have heard what is happening now, and I have not forgotten" (see Ex 6:4–5).

He repeats in verses 2 and 8, "I am Yahweh." Why does he continually name himself? It is because a person's name in that world was thought to define his character and nature. Here it speaks of presence, power, and passion. Since God is "I AM," there is no place where he is not. He is as much present in the brick pit as with the wheeling galaxies. Since he is "I AM," he is able to do what he wants. There are no limitations on him. Since he is "I AM," all of existence is derived from him and matters intensely to him. He is not mere, uncaring being. But what did all this mean for the Hebrews specifically? It meant that he was going to deliver them. Notice the three verbs in verse six: "I will *bring you out* from under the yoke; I will *free you* from the bondage, I will *redeem you*." What great promises! Thank God, he did what he promised, and he will do it, no matter what may befall us, in all the days to come.

Not only did Yahweh promise emancipation, he also promised adoption: "I will take you as My people" (v 7 NKJV). It is one thing to be free; it is another to belong. In the 1960s and 1970s, young people cut themselves loose from all the attachments that they felt limited their freedom to be themselves. But they discovered that life's meaning is found in attachments. Our lives have a sense of purpose and direction only when we belong to others. So God was not simply going to cut these slaves loose and leave them on their own. He was going to make them his people. I want that, don't you? I want to be God's man. I want to be able to call the Lord of the universe my Father (see Rom 8:14–17).

But Yahweh goes still farther: "Not only will you be my people, I will be your God" (v 7). Emancipation, adoption, and now consecration. Not only would they belong to Yahweh, but Yahweh would belong to them. The profound implications of that relationship are not spelled out here, but they would become clear later. For these people to be in an exclusive relationship with the one God of the universe, they had the privilege and the obligation of sharing his character ("You must be holy because I am holy" [Lev 19:2]). And all of that would issue in enlightenment: "You will know that I am Yahweh your God." Here we are again with the ultimate goal of the Exodus: to know who Yahweh is, and to know him in personal relationship. If you know God, if you know that he is your God, you can face anything. If you know your salvation is secure in God, you can survive anything. If you have the inner witness of God's Holy Spirit that he is your God and you are his person, you can have the courage to do anything.

The Romans sat open-mouthed when the Christians martyrs came into the arena .They were not dragged in screaming, but they marched in singing. The Romans said, "They must be drugged. They must not know that in just a few moments those iron bars will be lifted and roaring lions will rush out to tear them to shreds. They don't know." The Christians did know that, yet they knew something even better. They knew God, and they knew that on the other side of ten minutes of horror was an eternity of bliss. Oh, if you know that, you can face whatever comes rushing at you. You can face trouble. You can face loss. You can face shame. You can face anything if you know Yahweh.

## Moses' and the People's Response (6:9–12; 28–30)

So God told Moses not to give up. The overwhelming trouble that rolled upon Moses, the intensified crisis, gave God a perfect opportunity to show who he was. So Moses obeyed in spite of his doubts. We know he did because Exodus 6:9 gives us this matter-of-fact statement of courageous action: "So Moses spoke to the children of Israel."

No wonder God loved Moses: No fuss. No muss. Just, "God has said it; that's enough for me." Whatever had happened back there at Mt Horeb's burning bush, it had gotten through to Moses deeply enough that he was ready to follow when God spoke, despite his doubts and anxieties.

Unfortunately, it was not the same for the people. "But they would not listen to Moses" (6:9). Why not? "Because of their discouragement and harsh labor." I can imagine their protest, can't you? "Oh, no, Moses. We believed you when we thought that belief in God would not cost us anything. We believed you when we thought that following God would be all peaches and cream. We believed you when we thought there would be no pain or bloodshed or trouble in committing ourselves to God. But now we know that it costs something to follow God. No way!"

What about us? Let us confess that too often we're prone to respond to God as the Hebrews did. We say, "Yes, God, I am on your side," when we are walking on Easy Street. "Yes, God, I am on your side," when following him makes us look good. "Yes, God I am on your side," if it means that I'll always be financially and materially and physically better off for doing it. But we don't want God to put us through anything hard in order to show us who he is. You see, we don't want to experience God's *presence* as much as we want his *presents*. We want God's blessings. We want his gifts. But when the heat's on, count us out. That is where the Hebrew people were.

I am afraid too much of the American church has the same low-commitment mindset. In effect, these churches say, "Come in and worship with us because we don't have enough money or enough people here to pay the bills. Come in and everything will be wonderful. It won't really cost you much, just a dollar or two a week." If serving God were that easy and painless, everyone would be doing it, wouldn't they?

But God says, "I am Yahweh and you must know that I am Yahweh." The most priceless thing in all eternity is to know him as the one true God. Whatever the costs along the way, whatever the bloody footprints up Calvary's mountain following Jesus, whatever the cost, the end of the way is worth it all to know God—to know him as he really is. The Hebrews weren't willing to do that yet.

Their response discouraged Moses. When God told him in verse 10 to go back to the Pharaoh and demand again that he free the Israelites, Moses responded that it was pointless: The first time the people had received the message joyfully, but Pharaoh rejected it. Now the people had rejected it, so was Pharaoh likely to be more favorable? Hardly! A sign of the depth of his discouragement is that he again pleads that he is not able to speak well ("I am a man of uncircumcised lips").[2]

## Moses and Aaron's Genealogy (6:13–27)

When we look at verses 28–30 at the end of the chapter, we find a virtual repetition of 6:11–12: "Yahweh spoke to Moses in Egypt, saying, 'I am Yahweh. Tell Pharaoh, King of Egypt, everything that I tell you. But Moses said to Yahweh, 'Behold I am a man of uncircumcised lips. Why would Pharaoh listen to me?'"

Why would the same statements be made twice, on either side of a genealogy? This seems peculiar. I suggest that this genealogy establishes who Moses and Aaron are. But we already know that, do we not? In 2:1, we were told that Moses and Aaron were descendants of Levi, one of Jacob's sons. So what is the point of giving us this detailed information, and why here? I think it is given to establish once again that what is happening is not some accidental event or series of events. Moses and Aaron are the inheritors of God's promise. These are the descendants of Abraham, Isaac, and Jacob, and they are being delivered because God is faithful.

So when Moses says that it is fruitless to talk to Pharaoh, God says in effect, "Remember who you are. Remember where you have come from. Remember who I AM." Memory of our covenant identity makes all the difference in the world when we face

---

2. It is tempting to associate the phrase "uncircumcised lips" with Isaiah's cry in Isa 6, where he spoke about having unclean lips. Such an association would suggest that there is a flaw in Moses' dedication here, that he has not really surrendered his lips to God. But that does not seem to be what the context is saying. While the term *uncircumcised* can be used for what is spiritually unclean, it can also refer to what is defective. So it seems that Moses is not saying, "I have never surrendered my mouth to you"; he had. Rather, the comment implies, "My mouth is defective; it does not work very well." God's answer to that was, of course, Aaron.

impossible situations. We are not given our marching orders out of the blue; our calling is not ad hoc. We go as the representatives of the God who has been faithful, is faithful, and will be faithful. So we are told in 6:26 at the end of the genealogy, "These are Aaron and Moses *to whom the Lord said...*" (italics added). In other words, these men are not just accidental players on the stage of history; they are a central part of God's plan.

We do not always see God's plan and purpose in our own lives. Someone has said, "Hindsight is 20/20." It is easy looking back to see where God has led and how he has brought us through. But when we are in the middle of it, we have to walk by faith and say, "The God who is leading me today is the God who has led me in the past. The God who is offering his promises to me today is the God who has kept his promises in the past. The God who says he will be faithful today is the God who has been faithful all along the way." That is what Moses and Aaron had to say at that frightening moment.

One other thing we should note about Aaron's presence in this genealogy: God could have performed a miracle with Moses' mouth. He could have said, "Now, Moses, I am just going to stop that problem right now. You are never going to have this speech problem ever again." But he chose not to. He said, "No, here's the plan: You talk to Aaron, and Aaron will talk to the people and to Pharaoh." God may have another way of handling our problem that is just as good, just as effective, just as valuable as ours—even better! Sometimes we Christians have a lust for miracles. We pray, "God, I have this problem and here is how you must solve it. Solve it just like this." That attitude makes God my servant, functioning at my command. Do we really expect him to respond with, "Yes, sir"? Sometimes it seems that way, but that is not faith. It's presumption. Faith says, "O Lord, here I am. You know my need.

I want to serve you, I want to be the person you made me to be, and I give myself so you can use me, whatever and however." Then God may do a miracle if he chooses, or he may solve our problem in a more prosaic way as he did here. Instead of curing Moses' speech impediment, or whatever the problem was, God said, "I'll deal with your problem in my way and my time. I give you Aaron, so get going. Get going."

## Questions for Personal Study or Discussion

1. Why did the pharaohs make such elaborate burial monuments for themselves? How would the loss of Hebrew slave labor affect Egypt's religion?

2. "God's world is so made that our choices are more and more predetermined by the choices we have already made," Dr. Oswalt says. Give several examples of how this is illustrated by the life of Moses. Apply the same principle to Pharaoh; how do you see it confirmed in his life?

3. Has there been a time in your life when you have been tempted to disobey God because of discouragement? What happened?

4. Dr. Oswalt suggests that believers may have more difficulties after they commit their lives to Christ because "soldiers who raise their heads will be targeted." Do you agree? Do you see any proof of this in your life or the lives of other Christians you know?

5. Highly significant is the fact that God reveals himself in time and space; he did so in Egypt, and he still does. What evidence of this do you see in your own life?

6. How might you use your experience to lead someone else into a personal relationship with God?

# CHAPTER 5

# The Plagues
## (7:1–12:36)

Thus far in the study, we have looked at how God prepared his people for deliverance. We turn now to the actual events of deliverance. These events are described in two parts. The first is a series of disasters that fell upon Egypt because Pharaoh was determined not to lose his labor force (and, more than that, not to admit that there was some God greater than he). We know these disasters as "the plagues." The second part of the event narrative is found in Exodus 12:37–14:31, which describes the Hebrews' journey to and across the sea.

## The Purpose of the Plagues

As I have said several times above, God's purpose was not merely to get the Hebrew people out of Egypt. His primary purpose was that they should know him as Yahweh, the one true God. He took them through the experiences of deliverance to convince them that he is "the I AM" because, in knowing him, their freedom from bondage would have meaning. If they had gotten out of Egypt without knowing Yahweh, they would simply have gone from one kind of bondage into another. So the first purpose of the plagues is to make it unmistakably clear to God's own people that he is the only God and there is no other. Deliverance apart from an intimate knowledge of the Deliverer is not really deliverance.

We need to remember this fact each time we pray. So often, prayer is nothing more than a recitation of needs. But do we ever pray, "Above everything else, Lord, let me know you"? We see Paul thinking in this way when he says, "I have had everything and I have been through everything; but it is all worthless compared with the wonder of knowing Christ" (Phil 3:4–8). That is what God is saying to the Hebrew people here in the book of Exodus: "Above everything else, you need to know me, and in knowing me, you will receive my promises."

If anyone is to know that Yahweh is God, they must learn that what the world calls gods are not genuine gods. So the plagues were designed as an attack on Egypt's gods, as we are told in 12:12: "I will pass through the land of Egypt on that night, and will strike all the firstborn in the land of Egypt, both man and beast; and against all the gods of Egypt I will execute judgment. I *am* the LORD" (NKJV). That statement comes in the context of the last plague, which was a sort of capstone. It is God's response to the implied question, "What have you been doing, God, in all these plagues?"

"I have been executing judgment on the gods of Egypt."

To know Yahweh is to learn that he is a different order of being from all other so-called gods. So the plagues of Exodus were designed to teach Israel and Egypt that Amon is no god, Re is no god, Isis is no god, Osiris is no god. Yahweh is God and there is no other. We see this confirmed when we note the number of times that the word know is repeated in the context of the plagues:

7:5    "The Egyptians will know that I am Yahweh."

7:17   "Thus says Yahweh, by this you will know that I am Yahweh."

8:10   (Moses, talking to Pharaoh:) "Let it be according to your word that you may know there is none like Yahweh our God."

8:22   "I am going to set apart the land of Goshen, where the Hebrew people live, in order that you may know that I am Yahweh in the midst of the land."

9:14   "So that you may know there is none like me in all the earth."

9:29   (Moses, talking to Pharaoh:) "That you may know that the earth is Yahweh's."

10:2   "So that you may tell in the hearing of your son and your son's sons, the mighty things I have done in Egypt, and my signs which I have done among them, that you may know that I am Yahweh."

Seven times in the space of three chapters, we read that God sends the plagues so that people might know there is only one I AM, only one transcendent God, whose existence is entirely within himself, dependent on nothing outside himself. As we noted earlier, Scripture repeats certain statements in order to make a point. Yahweh repeated himself pretty extensively here, did he not? What was he saying? "I am doing these things so that you may learn that there is no other God."

This is not merely ancient history. We people of the twenty-first century can easily become practical idolaters. Of course, we do not believe that there is a literal god Amon or a god Re, but we tend to act as though the forces they represent are controlling our lives. How easy it is to act as though God is some place far away—not involved, not caring, not able to deal with the affairs of our lives—so we go through each day doing what has to be done, trying to manipulate the forces of nature and society in his absence. But the fact is, "I am Yahweh, the one and only I AM." How would our behavior and attitudes be different if we really believed that?

### The Nile

The first plague was upon the most beneficent deity, the deity upon whom Egypt's existence depended, the Nile goddess. Traditional history says Egypt is "the gift of the Nile." If the Nile River did not exist, there would have been no Egypt and no Egyptian culture. The Nile River extends for nearly a thousand miles to the Mediterranean, and down that valley flows life-giving water. Literally, you can stand in Egypt with one foot in the desert and the other one in a lush wheat field. Life goes just as far as the irrigation water of the Nile reaches, and where that water stops, death reigns. South of the Nile Delta, the habitable land of Egypt is literally three hundred miles long and ten miles wide. On either side is howling desert.

So the Egyptians knew that their life depended upon the Nile. They pictured her as a buxom, broad-hipped woman who carried life within her. But God said, "The Nile doesn't give you life." So Moses extended his rod and the life-giving Nile water turned to death-dealing blood. The Nile does not hold life in her hands; the

Lord holds life in his hands. That was the first lesson God taught through the plagues: "Don't look to a river for your life. Don't look to the world of nature, as beneficent as it can be. Yahweh is the one who holds life."

Interestingly, the Egyptian magicians were able to duplicate this miracle (7:22), just as they were able to duplicate Moses' turning a rod into a snake and back again. They were also able to duplicate the second plague, the infestation of frogs (8:7). But when Yahweh sent the third plague, the plague of gnats, they made a very interesting admission. They told Pharaoh, "We can't do this one; this is the finger of God" (8:19). Essentially, they admitted that their earlier "miracles" were trickery, sleight of hand. "But now," they said, "this is no longer in the realm of magic; this is God, so it is beyond our powers."

The situation got even worse for the magicians. By the sixth plague—the infestation of boils—not only were they unable to duplicate it, but they themselves suffered it (9:11). God clearly demonstrated that all the magic powers in the world, all the sorceries, all the artful techniques to manipulate nature, are nothing compared to the almighty power of God. We in the twenty-first century need to remember that. We live in a time of increasing darkness; when the principalities and the powers are more obvious around us. I believe there has been a kind of spiritual covering over the United States for the last one hundred and fifty years, because of the Great Awakenings on the frontier; but now that covering is being shot full of holes and the powers of darkness are beginning to reemerge. In this atmosphere, it is easy for us Christians to live fearfully and anxiously. "What's going to happen next?" we ask as we read news of the latest terror attack or natural disaster. But God says, "Don't fear those forces. Fear me, and you need fear nothing else." All the powers on earth are nothing compared to the power of God.

## The Frogs

The Egyptians were as polytheistic as any people in the world, except perhaps the modern Hindus. How tragic: two of the greatest of civilizations of history worshiping everything that moves. Two kinds of animals that the Egyptians worshiped especially were reptiles and the amphibians, because these creatures seemed to be able to live in two worlds simultaneously. The Egyptians were very interested in that. (As I said in chapter 1, Egyptians were anxious that the next world be at least as good as Egypt.) So they had a goddess of the crocodiles, as well as many snake gods and goddesses. But Yahweh said of the frog god, "The frog does not know the secret of eternal life. Only the I AM holds that secret. Apart from me, the frog is only a nuisance." So the frogs came out of the river and over the land. They were in the beds, in the cupboards, everywhere. And then they died, they died in heaps, so that the land stunk. Who is the Lord? The frog god? No. It is Yahweh, the God of the Hebrews, the god of whom Pharaoh says, "I don't know him and I won't serve him."

## Go Out to Worship

At this point it is worthwhile to think about a feature common to several of the announcements of the plagues that Moses and Aaron made. It was present in their very first demand (5:1) and several times later (8:1, 20, 25–28,; 9:1, 13; 10:4, 8–9, 24–25). This was their assertion that the Israelites wanted to leave Egypt in order to worship Yahweh. To many modern readers, this seems a bit disingenuous. Why didn't Moses just admit that he was demanding that Pharaoh free his slaves instead of this mumbo-jumbo about going off to worship for three days (5:3)?

First of all, Pharaoh understood the implications of this request quite well. If his slaves were allowed to go northward from the delta into the desert for three days, they were not coming back! But secondly, there is a certain logic in the increasing specificity of this request. Pharaoh kept thinking that he could finesse his permission in such a way as to grant their request and still hold on to them—not unlike all of our attempts to have God's blessings while we keep control of our own lives. Every time the Pharaoh toyed with those options, the penalties got worse. Eventually, there was no option left but abject surrender.

But I would like to suggest a third aspect of this request: Worshiping God in the desert really was the immediate purpose of the Exodus. It is no accident that the book of Exodus ends with a repeated description of the tabernacle. The Israelites' alienation from God was their deepest problem. If Israel had simply marched up the coast road for eleven days and walked into Canaan without ever encountering God in worship and surrender at Sinai, I doubt we would have heard anything more of them, and human history would have been profoundly different. So I believe Moses and Aaron's request to be set free to worship God was no elaborate subterfuge. It was what they had to do, and they knew it.

### Insects

The Bible does not say exactly what kind of insect was involved in the third plague. (The Hebrew people seem to have been much like my wife in this respect: They did not have a lot of different words for different bugs! To the Hebrews (and Karen) a bug is a bug is a bug, and the main thing about a bug is to kill it. So some translations say "lice" were the third plague, while others say "gnats." No translation has yet been daring enough to be really colloquial and just say "bugs"! In any case, the Egyptians worshiped the insect world, again because of its apparent power to turn death into life. They gave special devotion to the scarab beetle. They modeled beetles in stone as little oval amulets that they wore. They also put them in the mummy wrappings. Why? Because the scarab is a dung beetle. It makes a little ball of manure and buries its eggs in it, and then it pushes this little ball around until life comes out of the manure! Now who wouldn't worship a bug that could turn manure into life?

Similarly, flies were sacred to the Egyptians because they also could turn manure into life. They turned decaying flesh into life. Just turn over a dead piece of meat and you will find it is crawling with life. To be sure, it is a rather slimy, horrible life, but pretty soon full-fledged flies come out of it. Surely you have to worship that kind of power, the power to turn death into life. But God said, "Bugs don't have the key to life; the flies, the gnats, the scarabs are only created things. Yahweh is the one who holds life and death in his hands. He is the one you should worship. Don't believe that any created thing has produced the life that is found in it. Life originates and is perpetuated in one place alone: the heart of I AM."

This reveals a peculiar principle at work in both the Egyptian and the Hindu religions: Once people turn their backs on the glory of the transcendent God and start believing that life is in this world, they worship lower and lower life forms. This is exactly what the apostle Paul was inspired to say in Romans 1. When you begin to seek God in this world, you are driven lower and lower and lower, until you think the secret of life resides in fly eggs buried in a manure pile. But worshiping God takes you in the other direction. Worshiping the Lord God lifts you higher and higher and higher, appreciating the most complex forms of life and its most sophisticated expressions. I think it is no accident that the greatest music of the world was written for the church. It is no accident that the greatest art of the world was painted and drawn for the church. Something about lifting your eyes to the transcendent God lifts you out of the dung heap to set your sights on the glories of this earth and of the earth to come.

## The Animals

From the Nile, the frogs, and the insects, we move to the animals. The Egyptians worshiped the most powerful expressions of the animal world, particularly the goat, the ram, and the bull. These sexually potent animals—with their strong muscles, their ability to knock down their enemies, and their ability to get the female with young—surely they represent life, the Egyptians thought. Of these three, the bull was especially worshiped; it was the living image of Amon-Re, the Egyptians' high god. The Egyptians could say that Amon-Re was invisible, but in the same breath, they could say that he was present in that sacred bull.

We might say, "Wait a minute. He is either invisible or visible. He can't be both at the same time." But they would respond, "Oh yes, he can." Here we see the most fundamental distinction between the biblical understanding of reality and the nonbiblical understanding (and there really are only two). The nonbiblical view of reality says there is no distinction between god and the world; god is the world. So there is no distinction between what is and what is not, between the visible and the invisible, or between right and wrong. So Amon-Re is a bull and is not a bull at the same time. The biblical understanding of reality is diametrically opposite: God is not this world, and there is a hard and fast distinction between him and it. In the same way, there is a clear distinction between what is and what is not, what is seen and what is unseen, between right and wrong. These two views were crashing against each other in Egypt in those days. Once you say, "Yes, god is the world, though he is also more than the world," you are locked into idolatry, sorcery, and manipulation. Worst of all, you live in terror, because who can trust the vagaries of this world?

So Yahweh had said the Nile is no god, nor the frogs, nor the bugs. Now he said that Amon-Re, the bull god, was no god, either. That is in spite of the fact that the Egyptians were very serious in their bull worship. When a sacred bull died, he was carefully mummified. As a result, we have virtually all of them today—more than two thousand bull mummies! We have very few of the Pharaohs' own mummies, but we have all of the Pharaoh's bulls. But bulls were no god, and they did not have the secret of life.

I like to imagine that morning when the high priest of Amon-Re went out to worship Amon with his morning bale of hay. "Good morning, Lord Amon," I can hear him say. "Good grief, Amon! You are covered with boils! Who did that to you?"

And what would the bull have said if he could talk? "Yahweh. Yahweh did this to me. I am not the Lord of life, you silly man. I'm just a bovine animal. I am not the Lord."

Then the high priest of Amon would have looked at himself and seen the same boils on his arm that were on Amon-Re's back, and he would have wondered, "Who did this to me?" Had he paid attention, he would have heard a voice deep from within himself saying, "Yahweh did! These animals are not God. How dare you think that God is a four-legged animal?"

### Vegetation

Then there is the vegetation. Surely vegetation knows the secret of life: It keeps dying and sprouting up again. So the Egyptians worshiped the vegetation. Their god of vegetation was named Osiris. According to myth, Osiris was caught one day by his enemy brother, the god of the desert, who cut him up into little pieces. Then he shipped the pieces all over Egypt—a foot here, an arm there, and so on—but Osiris' consort, Isis, traveled all over the land and found the pieces of his body. She carefully put the pieces back together, buried them in a mummy case full of dirt, and set the mummy case out in the sun. Lo and behold, when they opened the mummy case after three days, Osiris had come back to life. (Oddly enough, he looked a lot like a wheat plant this time.)

In Egyptian art, Osiris was a mummy with a green complexion. He was the god who died every fall and rose every spring. He could be cut up, crushed with a flail, and sent all over the land; but if you planted him next spring, up he would come again. So the Egyptians told themselves that Osiris was the god who could take them through death and into life. But Yahweh said, "Don't you believe it."

So hail fell, breaking the plants down and stripping away their leaves. The Egyptians wailed, "Osiris, what happened to you?" But then they remembered that the spelt and the barley had not come up yet, so Osiris would still prevail. When the spelt and the barley came up, though, Yahweh sent grasshoppers to strip Osiris to the stalk.

Life does not come from plants, any more than it does from animals, insects, amphibians, or the Nile River. Life is only to be found in I AM. Apart from him, there is only death.

### The Sun

"Ah," the Egyptians would have said, "the failure of all those other gods is not fatal. For behind all of them stands the infallible sun. There is the ultimate source of life!"

As I said in the introductory chapter, it almost never rains in Egypt. About three hundred and sixty-three days a year, the sun shines there. Every morning, he jumps over the horizon and sails serenely across the sky in his boat, to dock at night in the west. The Egyptians believed that Re, Horus, Amon-Re, or whatever the sun was called, was the ultimate life giver. Take away his light and we die, so surely he is the one worthy of worship.

And Yahweh said, "Did you know that Re can be switched on and off?"

So in the middle of the day, the sun went out. Can you imagine the terror in the Egyptian people's hearts? "Who did that? Who shut off the sun?" It was the God of the Hebrews, Yahweh. And to make the lesson inescapable, the Hebrews had light when the Egyptians didn't (10:23). Without a doubt, Yahweh is the source of light and life, not Amon-Re. Yahweh is God and there is no other.

### Life

When we come to the heart of ancient Egyptian religion, we find that they worshiped life itself. Have you seen the little amulet that some people wear? That symbol of the *ankh* was very popular in the 1960s, although not so much now. The ankh looks like a cross with a loop on the top of it, and that is the Egyptian symbol for life. When you come to the bottom line, the Egyptians worshiped life. They thought, *If we can just go on living, if we can just transfer this life into the other world, from generation to generation, all will be well.* So ultimately, life itself was their god.

I daresay that is very much where we are in twenty-first-century America. Human life is god. We believe that if we can just perpetuate human life, we will have it all. A good deal of the current health craze is rooted in this unconscious worship of health and physical fitness. "What else is there to live for?" people say. "My kids? No way. I've got to jog. My job? No, I've got to work out on my Nautilus." Of course, some exercise is a good thing, as Paul says. But when it becomes an obsession, as it has for more than a few Americans, we become like the Egyptians. We act as though the maintenance of physical life is everything. My life is mine, and my priority is to perpetuate it. I can't let anything get in the way of that.

But when you have done it all, what do you have left except arthritic knees and tennis elbow? When you have tried every fad diet, what have you got? A flat stomach that's eighty-two years old. God makes the futility clear in that horrible climactic moment of Exodus, when the firstborn, the carrier of life to the next generation, dies: "Hear me, I am the Lord of life. I am the Lord of death. Your life is in my hands, not yours." That is what Jesus meant when he told the parable of the rich fool in Luke 12. *Hey, I've got it all,* that fellow thought. *I've got the best crop in thirty years. Build more barns to hoard it. I'll live off the interest.* And God said, "You fool. You will live off nothing. You are dead."

There is no God but the Lord. There is no Lord but Yahweh. There is no God but the God of Abraham, Isaac, and Jacob. To the world, this seems crazy. People convince themselves that there are many gods. Everybody is a god. There is nothing new about the so-called New Age Movement; it is a rather flabby version of the old Egyptian religion and the somewhat more modern Hinduism. Hinduism says we can all be gods. Oh, I like that. Hinduism says you can ultimately control your bodily functions for yourself. Oh, I like that. Hinduism says ultimately there is no god beyond your own mentality. You are Shiva; you are Krishna. I like that. But God says, "Sorry, it is not true. You are not god, and you never will be. I am the Lord. My child, I offer you life, but you have to reach out and surrender your own life in order to receive it." That is tough. I do not like that. I do not like giving anything away. But

God says through the Egyptian plagues, "Nothing in this world is ultimate; no created thing is god." So if we want to know the secrets of life and death, we must look beyond this world to the One who graciously reveals himself to us.

This is important for us to hear. We Christians believe that the Source of life is utterly other than this world, and unless the Source of life breaks in and shows himself to us, we will never find life. That is why the Bible is so critical, because it records how God has finally broken through to show us who he is. If this book is not reliable, then all is lost. Nature may suggest to us that God is powerful and beautiful, and in many ways he is, but that is not enough. Nature cannot tell us that God is the rewarder of them that seek him. It cannot tell us that there is only one God. It cannot tell us that God is love. It cannot tell us that God is completely reliable. It cannot tell us that God has a single moral standard. It cannot tell us the way to find eternal life. That is why the Bible is so critical to our daily lives and why it is so tragic when our pulpits descend to a message derived from the newspaper. There is no life except in the revelation of God, which breaks through to us from Scripture.

I am not suggesting that we should make the Bible some sort of magic talisman that we should carry in our pockets to avoid having any trouble. The Bible is no good to you unless you read it, and reading it is no good to you unless you obey it. There is no magic in the ink, paper, or binding. But in its truth, there is life forevermore, and there is no other place where God has revealed this truth except in the Word.

So if we ask why God performed all those plagues, he responds, "So that you would know me." You see, these people had lived in paganism for four hundred years. They had lived in the middle of the most lush, complicated paganism the world had ever produced. If there were no Bible and we human beings had to sit down and say, "Well, what is God?," what other source of information would we have but this world? What else but our own biological instincts and drives? If we had to work from that base, the results would look very much like ancient Egyptian and modern Hindu religion. The Egyptians were not polytheists because they lacked intelligence. They were because they refused the light that God was giving them and insisted on expressing the divine in terms of this world.

It should not surprise us at all that America is headed back to Egyptian and Hindu polytheism as fast as it can go. Once you reject the light, what else is there? If someone had said fifty years ago that Americans would be worshiping Satan, worshiping animal spirits, or trying to let dead persons of the past speak through them, the public would have laughed itself sick. We Americans are too bright for that. We are too scientifically sophisticated for that. We know that there is no spirit world.

Well, now we know better, just as the Hindus and Egyptians knew better. Of course there is a spirit world; anybody with brains can figure that out. So if a spirit world is part of this world, and if you intend to manipulate this world, you had better learn how to manipulate the spirits. That is just common sense, and we Americans are very commonsensical. So we are headed as fast as we can go back to the best that human wisdom could produce— five thousand years ago!

But God says, "I want you to know me. I want you to know the one God who is not the Nile, not the frogs, and not the sun. I want you to know the one God who is not even life itself, but who is more than all of these and holds them all in his hands. Then I would give these things to you as gifts for your enjoyment, use, cultivation, and care."

*Passover*

So the night came when the death angel was to pass through the land. Remember that God had exempted the Hebrews from many of the earlier plagues. He had said, "It will be dark in Egypt, but up there in the Delta, it won't be dark. The locusts will land on Egypt, but they won't land on the Hebrews." He simply exempted them. But with this plague, God does not say, "The death angel is not going to come here." Instead he tells the Hebrews, "The death angel is coming here too, and you need to be ready."

You see, this plague was different. What is the real thing from which the Hebrews need to be delivered—and from which all humans need to be delivered? It is death. Egypt is not the Israelites' enemy; death is. Now God says, "To be delivered from your ultimate enemy, it is not possible for me simply to say, 'It's not going to happen to you.'" Why not? Because to exempt certain people would be unjust. All of us have sinned and the wages of sin is death. So if God were to say, "I am not going to give my people their wages, but I will give them to others," that would be unjust. The world would fall to pieces in a moment, because the law of cause and effect is the very groundwork of our existence. So God said, "I cannot exempt you from death, because you have earned it. Death is deserved, richly deserved, by every human being. But I don't want you to die."

Well, God, what are you going to do?

"Take a lamb—perfect, spotless, unblemished, innocent—and slit its throat and splash the blood on your doorpost."

Death is the enemy of all humankind and God has made a way of escape. Every April for fourteen hundred years, believing Jews sat down at the table and the youngest person said, "Father, why do we do these things?" Then the father stood and said, "Children, we were slaves in Egypt, but God sent his paschal lamb, his Passover lamb, that we should not die on that night when the mighty Egyptians died. He passed us over, and we eat this lamb to remember our God and to praise his name." For fourteen hundred years, every April, they remembered: God has made a way of escape.

Passover does not celebrate the Exodus. That is surprising to some people, but the fact is that the Passover meal celebrates our deliverance from death. There is the real enemy. All of us have our Egypts from which we look for deliverance, but those things are not our real enemy—death is. Yet God has made a way of escape, and it is not merely a ritual symbol.

You see, it is no accident that Jesus Christ was crucified during Passover week, or that the last meal he ever shared with his disciples in a mortal body was a Passover meal. On that night when Jesus ate the roasted flesh of the lamb, all that Passover had been pointing to for fourteen hundred years came to its fulfillment.

I wonder if Peter looked at John during that meal and said, "John, something strange is going on here."

If he had, John would have replied, "Peter, I think you're right. But what is it?"

I suspect that about fifty days later, a day or two after Pentecost, as Peter and John were sitting together and rejoicing in what it meant to be filled with the Holy Spirit, Peter whacked John on the back, nearly knocking him off his chair. "John, that's what Jesus was doing that last night!" he could have exclaimed. 'Jesus was saying he is the lamb. His blood was put on the doorposts of our lives. His blood was shed for us, not that of some stupid lamb. That's what he was saying!"

In other words, the Passover was God's way of saying, "I have found a way to satisfy my justice and my love at the same time. Death has called for you and I have answered the call. Life is not in anything in this world. It is a gift from the I AM, your Creator and your Redeemer. I am the Lord who says, 'I have given my life for you, that death may never hold you in bondage.'"

Like so many of us, the Egyptians were trapped in the clutches of this world. Like them, we live in an age where it is almost impossible not to be worldly. I do not mean by that wearing the world's clothes or listening to the world's sounds. Rather, it is coming to believe, on an almost unconscious level, that things really are the most important. It means that how we look and what we think are most important. It means that getting enough to eat, enough to drink, enough sleep, and enough sex is all that anybody can hope for. That is worldly thinking, and we are surrounded with it.

Oh, how we need to hear God say, "None of these things are God. Not even life itself is God. I am God and I come with life in my nail-pierced hands to offer it to you"! Oh, let us return to our chart and compass, the Bible. Let us see again that God's kingdom is what matters. Let us go out to be in the world, but not of it, because we know he is the Lord.

# Questions for Personal Study or Discussion

1.  How many of the ten plagues can you recall from memory? If you had been an Egyptian peasant at the time, which of these plagues would have troubled you the most?

2.  Which of Moses' amazing "signs" were Egypt's magicians able to imitate? What do you think that proved?

3.  Dr. Oswalt describes the plagues as "a contest between God and the gods" of Egypt. How did these events discredit Egypt's pagan religion?

4.  Do you agree with Dr. Oswalt's observation that "powers of darkness are beginning to reemerge" in America? If so, give recent examples that you have seen.

5.  Scripture is one of the most important ways that God "breaks through" the spiritual darkness of our world. Have you experienced this in your own life? If so, share it with someone.

6.  "Passover does not celebrate the Exodus...but...our deliverance from death." Identify any parallels you see between the Passover and Jesus' death and resurrection. Some Passover symbols are roast lamb, bitter herbs, a cup of wine, and hidden bread.

7.  The Jewish Passover became the Christian ordinance we now call Communion or the Lord's Supper. In your own words, explain how Communion portrays our deliverance from death.

CHAPTER 6

# Out of Egypt and across the Sea
# (12:37–15:21)

In this chapter, we are continuing our study of the events of deliverance. With the revelation that life itself is in the control of Yahweh, Pharaoh was left with no alternative but abject surrender. Exodus 7:1–12:36 ends with the report that the Hebrews went out, taking much of the Egyptians' wealth with them, just as God had promised.

## Further Reflections on Passover and the Death of the Firstborn (12:37–13:16)

Interestingly, after a brief statement about their going out, the text circles back and begins to recapitulate some things about the Passover celebration. We are first given a historical description. (Here is how the Passover originated, how they first celebrated it, and what the consequences were.) Then the narrator seems to say, "Have you got that? Good. Now let's go back and review the implications of the Passover." Here's another example of repetition for emphasis, a favorite technique of the Exodus writer.

## The Feast of Unleavened Bread

The Passover was celebrated on one day, the fourteenth day of the month, which usually comes fairly close to April first for us.[1] For the seven days after that, from the fourteenth through the twenty-first, the Jews celebrated the Feast of Unleavened Bread. We find a description of this feast in 12:39 and again in 13:6–10. We are told that the Hebrews left Egypt with unleavened bread because, when the word came to go, they did not have time to mix leaven into the bread dough and wait for it to rise. So they set out with the unleavened bread they had.

There is an important theological implication here for us as Christians. We should not be so preoccupied with our daily activities that we are not ready to answer God's call at a moment's notice. The moving may be physical or spiritual, but we are called to be pilgrims, ready to move at a moment's notice. We need to maintain a loose hold on the details of our lives so we are ready to move. We should not be so attached to things that we have to "wait for the bread to rise" before we can do God's bidding.

There is another implication in the use of unleavened bread. In 12:15 we read, "Seven days you shall eat unleavened bread. On the first day, you shall remove leaven from your houses. For whoever eats leavened bread from the first day until the seventh day, that person shall be cut off from Israel" (NKJV). In some cases, an Old Testament reference to "cut off" actually means "killed." In other cases, that is not as clear, but it meant at a minimum that the person was excluded from the fellowship of God's people. That seems to be an extreme response to such a small matter as

---

1. Because the Jewish calendar is based on a lunar month of twenty-nine to thirty days, it slowly loses ground against the solar calendar, until eventually an extra month has to be added. This means that the date of Passover is never the same in the solar calendar from year to year.

this. What is so serious about having leaven in your house that you would be cut off from the people? It appears that God was trying to teach a weighty theological principle, which becomes clear when you study other references to leaven throughout the Bible. Over and over again, leaven is a symbol for sin. Like leaven, sin cannot be confined to a small part of our lives; very shortly, it contaminates the whole. Like leaven, sin will take the natural, fresh elements of life and ferment them. Like leaven, sin promotes decay and ultimately leads to death.

So I believe God ordained the Feast of Unleavened Bread in order to make a theological statement. In Passover, there is grace, free grace, and if you will be identified with God's people, that grace is yours. Enjoy it. But the single day of Passover is followed by seven days of the Festival of Unleavened Bread to emphasize that deliverance from the curse of death should lead to an ongoing life of freedom from sin, a life from which sin has been removed and in which it has no place. There in a nutshell is the whole biblical concept of salvation. Yes, we come into a relationship with God on the basis of grace alone and we remain in that relationship by grace alone. Even so, that grace should issue in a new kind of living. Why did God deliver us from the alienation of death? Why did God defeat the enemy of death in our lives? In order that we might live in festal fellowship with him without sin. That is to say, the Festival of Unleavened Bread reminds us that we might live without the leaven of sin in our lives.

No, deliverance from death is not an end in itself. That deliverance is intended to issue in a godly life, a life of holiness in which sin has no place.

On the first day of the Feast of Unleavened Bread, a Jewish family would go through the house hunting for leaven. Of course, the mother had already gotten rid of it all, except for one little package that she had hidden somewhere. So the whole family looked for that one last packet of leaven, to get rid of it so that the family could enter into God's festival. There ought to be times like that in our lives, when we say with the Psalmist, "Search me, O God, and know my heart… See if there is any wicked way in me" (Ps 139:23a, 24a NKJV).

*Participants in the Passover Celebration*
We find a second implication of this Passover service in the reference that no "foreigner" may eat it (12:43). However, verse 48 says that a stranger who lives in Israel and wants to keep Passover may do so on one condition—that he be circumcised. What is that saying? God's grace is free. God's deliverance from death is without price and without expense. It is true; there is no cost; you do not buy it; you do not earn it; you just rejoice in God's provision. You sit down at the table with your family and you partake of the lamb and of the saltwater and of the egg and of the cinnamon stick, all those things that for the Jewish people are loaded with symbolism, and you rejoice. It is free, but it is free to those who will identify themselves with the people of God.

There are no closet Christians, as there were no closet Jews. Salvation is free, yes, but it is free to those who say, "I choose to be identified with Jesus Christ. I choose to be identified with the people of God." I am not trying to receive his offering of himself while still playing my own game. I am not saying, "Yes, Lord, I want to look like a Gentile and live like a Canaanite, but I would also like to know that death has been defeated for me." But God says, "You can't do it that way." If you are going to experience the free grace of Passover, then you have to be publicly identified with the people of God. You have to say, "I have chosen to go his way. I have chosen the narrow way, and I am going to go that way."

I am glad this is the Christian era when circumcision of the heart is for both males and females. No longer do males only bear this mark of God and represent the females in their family. Now for every one of us, male and female, Jesus Christ comes and says, "Will you let me put my mark on your heart?" (see Rom 2:29; Col 2:11). Will you stand and be identified with Christ? Let your words and your whole demeanor of life say, "I am one of the crazy people. I am one who believes that God became flesh for me, and somehow God died in a moment of time for the whole human race. Yes, I am one of those people." Indeed, salvation is freely offered to everyone, just as Passover was freely offered to everyone. But these free gifts belong only to those who say, "I will be publicly identified with the people of God. I have made my choice, I will take my stand, and I don't care if it means that I look a little strange. I don't care if it means—and it may mean in America, within our lifetimes—bloody persecution. I don't care what it means, I am one of the people of God."

### The Firstborn

The third implication of Passover that God wants to make plain in the Exodus recapitulation of that event has to do with the firstborn. He says, "Every firstborn person and animal belongs to me. No, I did not kill them, I did not take their life, but precisely because I didn't, they belong to me, my hand is upon them. They belong to me." And so he says that every firstborn male animal must be sacrificed and every firstborn male child must be redeemed (13:15).

This clearly implies that life is a gift. As we saw in the previous chapter, the death of the firstborn was God's way of saying, "No, Egyptians, your life is not yours to hold onto. Life is not yours to give from one generation to the next. It can be lifted from your hand as easily as it was laid in your hand." And the same message is for the Hebrew people: "You do not produce life. I, Yahweh, do."

Do you remember the wonder you felt at your firstborn? There is a sense of awe, but there is also a certain sense of pride. That little life came from your two bodies! "Hey, Honey, we did that. We did that. Can you believe it? Some people said we could never do anything right. Well, just look at her!" But God says, "That's not your child, John. You and Karen didn't create life. You were participants, yes. But you did not make her; I did. She's mine, just as all life is mine."

If you are a good stock breeder and you raise prize-winning animals, you remember the pride you felt at the birth of that firstling. You held a perfect spotless young lamb in your arms and thought, *Man, I am a capable farmer. Look at what I've done!* But God says, "That lamb is not yours; it is mine. Life is a gift. Life is not something that you possess to use arbitrarily for yourself."

Every time a child is born first, every time an animal is born first, God says, "It is mine." All of the others—the second, the third, the fourth, the fifth, the sixth, the seventh, the eighth, the ninth, the tenth, the eleventh, the twelfth—belong to God too, but his special claim on the firstborn reminds me that they are all his gifts to me. All of them belong to him, but, in fact, he only asks us to redeem the first.

That thought relates to tithing as well. In his sermon "On the Use of Money," John Wesley said that we are not Old Testament people who think that only 10 percent of our money belongs to God. We are Christians, so we know better than that. We know that all of our money belongs to God. The only question for us Christians is, how much of God's money we are going to spend on ourselves? There is no stated percentage of giving for Christians, but we certainly cannot allow ourselves to fall below the standard named in the Old Testament. That is the floor from which we start. Real giving begins after that.

So the act of sacrificing or redeeming the firstborn says that all of life is a gift. We must use it in that way, as a gift from God, not as a possession of our own. But there is something more going on in those commands concerning the firstborn. Year by year, the Old Testament Jews sacrificed their firstborn lambs. Year by year, their firstborn children were redeemed by a special offering for the service of the temple. Year by year, and what happens?

How easy it is to begin to think that with my offering I have bought my life. I have bought my life by giving my firstborn ram. I have bought my life by redeeming my child. I have propitiated God by my efforts in sacrificing the firstborn. But a thoughtful person, Micah, says, "Shall I give my firstborn for my transgression, the fruit of my body for the sin of my soul?" (Mic 6:7 NKJV). Micah understood that no other creature, animal or human, can take my place before God. My sin demands my death. So God replies, "I am so glad you figured that out. Now let me tell you about my firstborn."

It is no accident that Jesus, the second Person of the Trinity, is twice referred to as the "firstborn" in the New Testament (Rom 8:29; Col 1:18). For a long time, I wondered about that. There aren't any "born" members of the Godhead. "The Word was with God, and the Word was God" (John 1:1 NKJV). Jesus is God, so why call him the firstborn? Then one day it dawned on me: Oh, it is because of the symbolism of the Passover. By giving himself in Jesus, it is as though God has given his firstborn on our behalf. The result is that you and I do not have to give our firstborn anymore. God has given his best instead. God has given the one who is life, so that indeed death is defeated forever. Thank God.

So back there in the Passover, in the death of the Egyptian firstborn and the life of the Hebrew firstborn, God was setting the stage for a momentous final Passover on Calvary. Thank God. Thank God.

## The Journey to the Sea (13:17–22)

With that recapitulation of what the Passover teaches us, the book of Exodus is ready to return to the story of the Hebrews' escape from Egypt. Immediately, we discover God doing something that seems very strange: Instead of taking them on the coast road, where it is about an eleven-day journey on foot from Egypt to Canaan, God led the people southeastward from their homes into the desert. As a result, it took them nearly a year and a half to reach the southern edges of the Promised Land.

What was going on? Was not God's primary purpose in leading the people out of Egypt to get them into Canaan? If you have been paying close attention through the previous pages, you are saying, "No, that was not God's primary purpose. It may have been his final purpose, but his ultimate purpose was that the Israelites should know God." God led his people on the exodus so that they would know that he is Yahweh, whether in Egypt or out of Egypt, whether in Canaan or out of Canaan. The whole point of the procedure was to make them aware of the personal presence of the Lord.

So God took them southeast into a desert area that would eventually open out into a collection of lakes and swamps known as the Reed Sea. Today, the Suez Canal goes through this area. In ancient times, it was an extension of the Gulf of Suez, which is in turn the northwest arm of the Red Sea.

Clearly, this is not anything like a direct route to Canaan; at best, it was a very long way around. All of us have probably experienced something like this in our lives. What we were going through did not make any sense in terms of what we thought God's purpose was for our lives. But later, we realized that in fact the long way around fitted precisely into God's larger purposes in our lives.

We come to a very interesting explanation of God's actions in 13:17: "Lest perhaps the people change their minds when they see war, and return to Egypt" (NKJV). In other words, God could have taken the Hebrew people to Canaan in an instant if he wanted, but the people did not know him well enough to withstand Canaan. There they would be surrounded by one of the greatest cultures of the ancient world. These farmers, shepherds, and bricklayers would confront military power. So if that happened right away, they would say, "We can't do this. Forget it. Get out. Back off." In fact, even after the experience of crossing the sea and the revelation of Sinai, they said something very like that at Kadesh Barnea (Num 14). How much more it would have been the case without those experiences. God was saying, "You don't know me well enough yet to trust me when you are faced with the Canaanite war machine. You don't know me well enough to believe when you face impossible odds. You don't know me well enough to walk into the hailstorm and know there is a roof over your head, a roof built by the Living God." So Yahweh led them out of Egypt the "wrong" way.

God does that in your life and mine. He leads us up to brick walls where we have to say, "This is impossible, God. I can't do this." You know, the greatest discovery any of us can ever make is, "I can't handle it." And the most damnable thought is, "Hey, I can do anything. I can handle it. I've never run into anything that I couldn't take care of."

That's what God was trying to teach Jacob for more than twenty years, but Jacob seemed to rise to every occasion. Yes, he needed a little help once in a while. (It is nice of God to help us out now and then, is it not?) But one night, as Jacob pictured the raging red face of his brother Esau, when Jacob had lost everything he possessed in a vain attempt to buy Esau off, he said, "God, you can't let me go. Don't leave me. I can't make it without your blessing. I can't make it without your touch upon my life, even if it cripples me. I need your touch." What a good night that was! And for every one of us, the best night of our lives will be when we lie flat on the ground and say, "Lord, this is impossible. There is no way out of this one. Lord, it's over. I can't do it anymore."

In that moment, God says, "Don't you understand, child? You don't have to do it. I can do whatever is necessary for you and through you and in you. Don't you understand?"

This is why God leads the Israelites in the wrong direction. Don't ever be unhappy about the wrong directions in your life, if they lead you to a place of total dependence upon God. Think what it would have meant for the Hebrew people not to be able to point back to the Red Sea. Throughout the rest of their history, they have said, "Do you know how we know we are the people of God? We stood at an impossible situation and God delivered us. If that doesn't prove we are the people of God, nothing will." So don't blame God for the hours of despair, disaster, and darkness in your life. Thank him. Praise him. Because in those moments, he can reveal your incapacity and his eternal, ultimate, divine capacity.

## Crossing the Sea (14:1–31)

Although they were led by a supernatural pillar of cloud and fire (13:20–22), the Israelites soon seemed to be blundering about aimlessly (14:2–3). That convinced Pharaoh that he had an opportunity to redeem himself from the disaster he had suffered. But in fact, it was the climactic opportunity for Yahweh to demonstrate that he alone is the I AM (14:4, 18). In current parlance, the outcome of Pharaoh's attack would be a no-brainer. A disorganized mob of refugees would be no match for what was, at that time, the ultimate military weapon. That weapon was the light, three-horse chariot carrying a driver and a bowman using a compound bow—a bow so powerful that it could drive an arrow through a copper ingot. These chariots were the ancient equivalent of modern tanks, and the Egyptians had the best chariot army in the world. The Israelites stood no chance at all against such a force, particularly since they were backed up against a body of water too big to go around and too deep to wade across.[2]

In such a situation, I suspect we might have said something very like what the Hebrews said: "Did you bring us out here to die because there weren't enough graves in Egypt? Were the cemeteries too full in Egypt, so you brought us out here to leave our bones in the wilderness? Moses, didn't we tell you to let us alone to be slaves to the Egyptians? Didn't we tell you to take your hand off us?" (see 14:11–12.)

Perhaps you have been in such a predicament recently, and you just wanted to say, "Lord, just let me alone. I'm tired.

---

2. While later passages in the Bible refer to crossing the "Red Sea," that is obviously a case of naming the part by the whole. As the Gulf of Suez is an arm of the Red Sea, so the Reed Sea was an extension of the Gulf of Suez. Exodus is consistent in saying the Hebrews crossed the "Reed Sea." What the Hebrews were backed up against was almost certainly one of the considerable lakes that were found in the area just north of Suez.

Everything has gone wrong. So Lord, just take your hands off of me." We do not like to admit that, do we? Even so, God the Father says, "No, I will not let you go. How can I let you go? You are my chosen child. I am going to stay with you."

"But God, it hurts."

"Keep your eye on the goal. Keep your eye on the end of the road and know that it is worth it all. Whatever the cost, whatever the price, whatever the pain, it is worth it all."

Perhaps you remember the story that is told of the great sculptor Michelangelo. Someone asked him, "How in the world do you create those gorgeous statues?" He said, "Well, I find a piece of rock where the angel is trying to get out, and I knock off everything that doesn't look like the angel." I suspect that if a rock could cry, it would have wept while Michelangelo was working it over with a hammer and chisel. It would have said, "Let me alone. Stop. That hurts!" But the sculptor persists, saying, "No, no, I see the angel in you that's trying to get out, so I am going to knock off everything that doesn't look like it."

In our case, the image of Jesus Christ is trying to emerge from our misshapen stone, so God has to knock off everything that doesn't look like Jesus. That hurts, as you know very well. Still, what alternative is there if we are ever to become what we were created to be?

Moses' response to all of this, as recorded in 14:13, is very significant. The Bible gives no clue that Yahweh had yet revealed to Moses what he planned to do the next day. So far as we know, Moses saw only what the people saw: an impassable sea in front of them and the world's greatest chariot army behind them. But Moses had learned the lesson of the plagues. Examine his words: "Do not be afraid. Stand still, and see the salvation of the LORD, which He will accomplish for you today. For the Egyptians whom you see today, you shall see again no more forever" (v 13 NKJV). "Be quiet, because Yahweh is going to fight for you" (v 14).

The Israelites must have wondered how Moses could say such a thing. "Look at that sea! Look at their army! Look at the realities!" But Moses would have replied, "Friends, I am looking at reality. I am looking at true Reality. I am looking at the One, compared to whom these things are whiffs of smoke."

Why is our faith so often weak? I believe it is because we stop looking at reality. We stop looking at the One who is Reality, and we fix our eyes on these passing, ephemeral things. We get mesmerized by things that are not reality at all. I do not mean to say for a moment that this is an unreal world, a shadowy reflection of some primeval world. This world certainly is real, but it is only real because Reality has chosen to invest it with some of his reality. But too often we look only at what is derivative instead of the Source, so we get confused. Oh, how we need to have our eyes upon Reality! "The Lord will fight for you, and you will hold your place" (14:14). I do not know what kinds of obstacles you are facing today or what kinds of armies are at your back, but I do know this: If you will fix your eyes on the ultimate Reality, you will be able to stand still in the middle of it and see a divine deliverance accomplished for you.

### The Historicity of the Crossing

At this point, let us consider the significance of the historicity of the crossing of the sea. Tragically today, it is not uncommon to hear well-meaning people (even well-meaning Bible scholars) say things like, "Well, we don't really know what happened in the exodus. Perhaps a few hundred people ran across a swamp and some Egyptian chariots got stuck in the mud, so the people thought that was the act of God. We just don't know what actually happened. In fact, there may not have been an exodus at all. That is not important. What is important is the wonderful truth that God loves us and cares about us, and that we can depend on God in our darkest hours."

Let us apply that same mindset to the New Testament for a moment: "We don't really know whether Jesus rose from the dead or not. Maybe he fainted and then revived, after having been beaten nearly to death. His followers could have pushed that two-ton stone away. In fact, his disciples may have hid his body, or perhaps some believing Jews. But really, none of that makes any difference. All that really matters is we have the faith of eternal life because of this wonderful story of the resurrection."

Such opinions raise two important issues that we must consider any time we study a historical narrative in scripture. First of all, if faith is not related to fact, it is not faith but delusion. A madman may well believe that he is Harry Truman, and construct his whole life around that notion. But we would not call his belief faith. Why not? Because there is no evidence exterior to that man's own delusion to support his belief. Suppose there had been no Red Sea crossing. Suppose that years later, when Canaanites asked the Israelites, "How do you know you are the chosen people of God?" they had responded, "Because God had our backs to the sea, and he led us across and delivered us in a mighty miracle." No one would consider that a wonderful example of faith, but a sad example of self-delusion. If someone creates an elaborate fiction to justify their belief, their belief is still just a fiction.

So if you and I say, "I am going to live forever; I am going to rise from the dead," based on nothing more than some legends about Jesus Christ, we are of all people most to be pitied. Either the tomb is empty or we are fools. There is no middle ground. By the same token, unless there was a historical exodus, unless there was a moment when God broke into time and space and delivered a nation from its enemies in a way which no humans could do, then the whole idea that the Hebrews are the chosen people of God is a fairy tale that we would be better off without. Likewise, are all those things I have said about God's power, trustworthiness, and love. They are all a delusion.

This leads us to a second observation: This is the fact that, outside of the Bible, there are no examples of people making up national historical sagas to explain and authenticate their faith. If we could find a lot of other examples in religious literature where people did that sort of thing, we might be forced to conclude that the Hebrews had done the same. But there are no examples of this phenomenon elsewhere. What does that say? It says that the Hebrews did not make up their nation's story because it was a common way to establish a new faith. It argues strongly that when the Hebrews, and the early Christians, say that they believe God because of the overwhelming, unsought-for, historical experience they had together, that is exactly what happened.

Yes, other peoples around Israel made up stories, but they were not about unique, nonrepeatable, national events in time and space. They were about unchanging cycles in some primeval world outside of our time and space, which are supposed to pre-condition what happens in this sad little reflection that came from nowhere and is going nowhere. That is not by any stretch of the imagination what Israel and the early Christians did. What they say is unlike anything to be found elsewhere in the world's religions.

So since we are convinced that the Bible does faithfully report a real historical event, we can use the biblical account to reconstruct exactly what happened, and all who examine the account will come up with the same reconstruction, right? Wrong. The Bible's reports are sketchy and incomplete. Why is that, if it is a report of a real historical event? Because the biblical account was not written to satisfy our covetous desire to know exactly how things happened to our ancestors. We are given enough details to know that it really did occur, but not so many that we can thoroughly document what happened. In this case, the nature of the account cannot possibly be squared with some tale of a few hundred people tiptoeing through a swamp. Waters that could not be waded through were divided on both sides for a great number of people to pass through, and when those waters returned, they drowned the foremost chariot army in the world at that time. That is for sure. But beyond those facts, the biblical writers do not think we need to know a lot more. Scripture focuses instead on what we can learn about God out of that event.

In many ways, this is precisely analogous to what the Bible does with Jesus. Without a doubt, Jesus Christ is described as a real human being who walked the dusty roads of Judea, Samaria, and Galilee. But what do we know about the day-to-day details of his life? What do we know about his physical appearance? The answer to both questions is: nothing. Why is this? Again, because the Bible's chief purpose is not to document and reconstruct human history but to reveal eternal truths that were demonstrated by these events.

## The Song of the Sea (15:1–21)

So what truths are we to learn from the events of deliverance, culminating in the crossing of the sea? Those lessons are summarized for us in a powerful way in Moses' great Song of the

Sea. This is one of the great songs of the Bible, standing with the Psalms and the songs found in the book of the Revelation.

In many ways, music is a mystery. How is it that we can make sounds through our vocal chords to form speech, but if we do the same thing in a slightly different way with differing tones and rhythms, it is song. What is the difference? Oh, physiologists and physicists can give us scientific explanations, but they still don't explain it. Nor do they explain the remarkable power music has over us. But when we come to grips with a marvelous reality, when we come to the place where we can stand in the midst of uncertainty, when we come to a place of security and hope, we burst into song. Song just springs up from within us to express the joy, hope, and peace that we know.

That is what happened here. It is not accidental that Moses was the one who uttered this song. He had dared to believe when all seemed hopeless, and so he felt exultant joy when that hope became reality. Undoubtedly, many of the Hebrew people were simply befuddled by the amazing turn of events, but not Moses. He knew what the stakes had been, and he knew what the outcome meant.

Like a great symphony, there are three movements in Moses' song. The first is found in verses 1–3, which we will title "My Saving God." The second movement includes verses 4–12 and may be titled, "Them and Thou." The last movement covers verses 13–18, "The God of *Hesed*."

## My Saving God

Notice the first-person pronouns in verses one and two: "I will sing to the LORD for He has triumphed gloriously! The horse and its rider He has thrown into the sea! The LORD is my strength and song, and He has become my salvation; He is my God, and

I will praise Him; my father's God, and I will exalt Him" (NKJV). What is the point? The first-person pronouns express that glorious moment when Moses knew Yahweh no longer as the God of the fathers but as the One whose saving power became an intimate, personal reality. Yahweh is not *their* God or *his* God, but *my* God. Oh, Moses had heard about him for years. He had heard the ritual Jewish testimonies that "he is my father's God," but a God who is only my father's God is of little importance to me. The moment has to come when, as wonderful as all those testimonies of the past have been, I know that he is my God.

The great danger of a good heritage is a kind of idolatry in which the God we worship is merely the God of our parents and grandparents. But is he your God? Do you know he can do the same miracles in your life that he did in the lives of your father and the mother in the past? Is he your saving God? Have you allowed him to do in your life what he wants to do? We dare not ask him, "Oh, do again what you did fifty years ago." We have to say to him, "Lord, do what you want to do with me today. Do what you planned to do today. Do it in your creativity and power, for your glory. Do something that will make what happened fifty years ago look small by comparison."

We are not asking God to recreate the past; we are asking the God who did glorious things in the past to demonstrate and reveal himself in our presence in such a way that we can say, "He is my God. He is my saving God."

What a time that must have been on the far shores of the Red Sea. Can you imagine? This is another one of those instant replays I want to see. Dancing and singing and laughing and, every once in a while, stopping to look at the sea and see some pieces of chariots floating around there. Here would come the dead body of a horse, and the Israelites would laugh and sing and dance, "We're alive, we're alive! We don't have Egyptian arrows piercing our breasts. We're alive!" No wonder people think Christians are crazy. We are alive. We are redeemed. Hell has no claim on us. Praise God. Praise God. He is our strength and song; he has become our salvation; he is our God. We praise him as our fathers' God, yes. He is the same God. But we exalt him because of what he's done for us. Thank God. Thank God!

### Them and Thou

As we move on to verses 4–12, we see an interesting moving back and forth between "them" (the Egyptians) and "Thou" (Yahweh). "Pharaoh's chariots and his army He has cast into the sea; his chosen captains also are drowned in the Red Sea. The depths have covered them; they sank to the bottom like a stone" (vv 4–5 NKJV). All the power of the human race is a bubble before God. "Your right hand, O LORD, has become glorious in power" (v 6 NKJV). I don't have to worry about "them" because I am fixed on "Thou."

Are there some overwhelming *thems* in your life now? Are some things bearing down on you so that you just don't know how you are going to handle them? You don't know how you are going to meet them? Take your eyes off "them" and get them on "Thou."

"In the greatness of Your excellence You have overthrown those [them] who rose against You; You sent forth Your wrath; it consumed them like stubble. And with the blast of Your nostrils the waters were gathered together; the floods stood upright like a heap; the depths congealed in the heart of the sea. The enemy said, 'I will pursue, I will overtake, I will divide the spoil. My desire shall be satisfied on them. I will draw my sword, My hand shall destroy them.' You blew with Your wind, the sea covered them." (vv 7–10 NKJV)

Whatever the Enemy says today is not very important, but what God does makes all the difference. The Enemy says, "I am going to delude them; I am going to divert them; I am going to destroy them; I am going to divide them." But God says, "No, you're not." That is good enough for me. My future is not up to "them"; it is up to "Thou."

### The God of Hesed

Moses sang, "You in Your mercy have led forth the people" (v 13 NJKV). The Hebrew word translated "mercy" here has a range of meaning for which there is no single English equivalent. It takes seven different English words to translate all that is in the one Hebrew word, *hesed*. The first letter is similar to a rough *h*, a sound that English speakers have a hard time pronouncing. Our babies produce the sound easily, but we lose it as we grow up because we don't have it in any English words. The KJV and later translations in that tradition translate *hesed* as "mercy" because the first translation of the OT from Hebrew into Greek had the same problem we have—no single equivalent capturing all the connotations—and settled on a Greek word meaning "mercy." That is not a bad translation, but "mercy" is only the tip of the iceberg, so to say. More recent translations use "grace," "love," "kindness," "lovingkindness," "steadfast love," "unfailing love," and "loyalty," among others, to try to capture other dimensions of what this Hebrew word conveys. It really takes a sentence to translate it: "the deep unfailing devotion of a superior to an inferior, especially when it is undeserved." About three-quarters of the 250 occurrences of the word in the Old Testament are used, as here, to refer to God. Interestingly, the word is unknown in any other Semitic language. It is as though the Hebrews have had to invent a word to express this amazing quality that they found in their God and in no other. We will encounter it again in what is its most formative setting, Exodus 34:6.

Here *hesed* leads us into the last stanza of the poem, in which Moses looks to the future. Moses recognizes that, just as none of what God has done in delivering Israel from Egypt was deserved, neither will be his eventual bringing of them into Canaan. This whole redemption story is an expression of God's undeserved, overflowing grace. Just as he overcame every difficulty in the past for love's sake, so he will overcome every opposition in the future. None of the neighboring peoples, such as the Philistines, Edomites, Moabites, or Canaanites, will be able to resist Israel. Instead, they will melt away in fear as Yahweh displays his gracious power through Israel (vv 14–15; see also Rahab's comments in Josh 2:9–11).

But besides the certainty of future victory because of God's *hesed*, there is another important aspect to this last stanza of the Song of the Sea, stated in verse 13. Where is God guiding his people? To his "holy dwelling." What is it that makes Canaan special? The fact that God has chosen that place to live with his people. Like the soil around the burning bush, there is nothing intrinsically holy about that land. The only thing that sets it apart as holy is the presence of Yahweh. Canaan is not special because it is to be Israel's homeland, a gift of God for Israel's independence. It is special because Yahweh has chosen it, and will make himself manifest to his people there. This same thought is picked up again in verse 17. Canaan is Yahweh's "inheritance" (note NLT, "special possession") first and then Israel's. It is his "dwelling," his "sanctuary." The thing that makes Canaan special, as Moses fully realized, was the presence of God (see 33:15–16). Without God's presence, Canaan was just one more unimportant parcel of dirt on the globe. But with that presence, Canaan was the most desirable spot on earth. As the psalmist was to say, "Your *hesed* is better than life" (Ps 63:3).

## Questions for Personal Study or Discussion

1.  Why did the exodus pilgrims take unleavened bread with them?

2.  Why did Jewish people remove all leaven from their homes during the Feast of Unleavened Bread (i.e., what did leaven symbolize)?

3.  In the ancient world, pagan people often sacrificed first-born children to their gods, while Jewish people made an annual temple offering on behalf of their firstborn. Imagine a conversation between a Jewish mother and a pagan mother who have just completed these rituals. What do the different requirements tell them about the gods they worship?

4.  Has God ever led you on a long, winding path to an important goal? What did you learn through that experience?

5.  Dr. Oswalt says, "Think what it would have meant for the Hebrew people not to be able to point back to the Red Sea." How might their relationship with God have been different, without that experience?

6.  Reflect on the story of Michelangelo, who resolved to "knock off everything that doesn't look like" a beautiful statue he visualized. Do you recall any habits, attitudes, or personality traits that God has "knocked off" in order to make you a better person?

7. After four hundred years of Egyptian life and a long, slow slide into heathenism there, the Israelites come back to Canaan because God intends to dwell with them there. Where are you especially aware of the presence of God? How might you spend more time there?

CHAPTER 7

# Revelation of Providence
## (15:22–18:27)

## The Nature of Salvation

Before we continue on in our study of the book, this is a good place to summarize what the first fifteen chapters have taught us about the nature of salvation. Four key things are taught in these chapters:

**1. The need for salvation** is a divine/human problem. In short, it is a human problem that creates a divine problem. For the Hebrew people to be in bondage in Egypt was a problem for God, because he had promised to give them the land of Canaan, so he could not leave them there. They were his people, and if he left them in bondage, the whole world would know that Yahweh was not true to his word. He had to deliver them.

The same thing is true for the whole human race. Our sin with its resulting shame and disaster is a divine problem. God cannot let us go. He cannot sit passively on the sideline, watching the people he made in his own image plunging into eternity without him. So when you feel yourself in the depths, remember that that is God's problem too. When you feel you have failed and wound up in the bondage of guilt and shame, that is

God's problem too. The need for salvation is a divine/human problem.

**2. The cause of salvation** is divine self-expression. What does such a statement mean? Think about it: What got the Hebrew people out of Egypt? It was God's making himself known, showing himself in his power and his glory to the world.

If the human race is ever to be saved, it will be because God expresses his nature and his character to the world. Does that sound complicated? Think of John 3:16: "For God so loved the world" that he devised a program? "For God so loved the world" that he reached down with a sky hook and jerked people out of their sin? No, nothing like that. What does Scripture say? "For God so loved the world *that he gave his only begotten Son.*" God saves us by showing up himself. He steps into our problem and helps us to recognize who he is and what he wants us to do in our lives. Salvation is the result of divine self-expression.

**3. The purpose of salvation** is that you may know Yahweh in an intimate, ongoing relationship. Haven't we seen this message breathing through the previous chapters? Why did Yahweh save his people? So that they might come into an intimate, personal relationship with him. Did he want to take them to Canaan? Of course. But why Canaan? Because that was where he chose to manifest himself to them, to "make his face shine upon them" (Num 6:25; see 15:12, 17).

That is why God saves us as well. Of course he does not want us to go to hell. He does not want us to spend an eternity without him. He does not want us to lose all that we were made for. And, yes, he does want us to go to heaven. But all of those are side issues. God saves us chiefly because he wants us to know him. If we truly know him, then those other questions are answered. Here we see how a nominal Christian misses the whole point of what Christian salvation is about. It is not about saying some formula, memorizing some Christian mantra, or performing a minimum of religious obligations. No, salvation is to know God—to know him personally.

Why did I go through the rigmarole of marriage? I wanted to know that girl. I was not interested in what she could do for me, as wonderful as all those things have been through the years. I was not interested in obtaining certain benefits. I wanted to share my life with her and have her share hers with me. If we accept Christ to avoid hell, to avoid guilt and shame, God is gracious and will take us on just about any grounds he can find. But what he is really after—the reason he let himself be nailed to the cross—is that we might know him, for in knowing him is eternal life.

**4. What is the outcome of salvation?** We will see this in more detail in chapters 19–40, but it is already here in germ in chapters 14 and 15. The outcome of salvation is obedience and worship. God said, "Get going. Head toward the Red Sea." So the people went, even if that seemed the wrong direction. They had experienced deliverance from the Death Angel and they had received the word from the Egyptian officials that they were now free to go, so they were ready to obey. Then, when they stood on the other side of the sea and looked at the wreckage of the Egyptian chariot forces, what else was there to do but to join Moses and Miriam in worship? That is what salvation is all about: obeying him because we know him and love him, and worshiping him because of who he has demonstrated himself to be in what he has done for us.

## The Wilderness

The first question of Exodus was, "Can God deliver?" It was answered with an unmistakable yes in chapters 1–15. Those chapters leave us with a certainty of God's power.

But the second question is, "Does God care?" Is he concerned with our basic human needs, or are those too petty and unimportant for him? Can we depend on him for the great issues of deliverance and destiny but still have to scrounge our daily needs by ourselves?

## Murmuring

It is amazing that within a few short verses of the great worship service on the shore of the sea, we see the people entering into a behavior that would be all too characteristic of them for the next forty years—complaining against Moses and Aaron, and ultimately against Yahweh himself. They do this again and again because they are afraid. They know that they cannot supply their most basic needs in that howling desert, so deep within themselves they do not trust God to do it either. In chapters 15–18, Yahweh demonstrates in unmistakable ways that he does care and that he can be trusted. He will provide water, health, food, protection, and even organization. Even though the Israelites did not really learn the lesson, it is clearly taught in these chapters nevertheless.

It is probably too easy for us to criticize the Israelites for their sudden descent from ecstatic worship to grumbling and complaint. The plain fact is that this kind of behavior is all too common for all of us. We have a great moment of spiritual experience, and then the difficult realities of life strike us in the face. At that moment Satan, the Accuser, steps in, leveling his accusation against God. "God doesn't really care," he says. "If God really cared, he wouldn't have let this happen to you. If God really cared, that would not have occurred in your life. If God really cared, he would make everything easy street. If God really cared, he would have taken you straight up the coast road with its easy stopping places. Instead, he has brought you into this stony, arid wilderness. If he even exists, he clearly doesn't love you."

Here Satan is appealing to a deeply idolatrous instinct in the human heart. If we are given the least chance, we will turn God into our idol—that is, a spirit being whose chief purpose is to take care of us and meet our needs as we understand them. So we tell God, "I know how you ought to take care of me. I know what you ought to do in my life, I know what your purposes ought to be for me, and I will tell you what they are and how you should do it. And if you don't do it, you don't love me." That is where they were. They did not know God. That is why Exodus 16:6 says, "In the evening you will know that the Lord has brought you out of the land of Egypt." They still did not really know Yahweh, did they? They knew his power but not his care. You see it again in Exodus 16:12: "In the morning you will be filled with bread and you will know that I am the Lord." They had seen God's negative power, his mighty ability to destroy the chains that bound them and break down the enemies' strongholds, but they hankered to see his positive power to bless them. To this God says, "You will know it. You will know it." Although God does not exist for humans, the Israelites would see ample proof that he is still pleased to use his power to provide for us. The issue is to let him choose when, where, and how that provision occurs.

If you have teenagers in your home, you know a good deal about murmuring, the disposition that questions and doubts everything. You say, "Do this," and the answer is, "Why?"

"Never mind why, just do it."

"Why should I never mind?"

Questioning and doubting—that's the typical teenage attitude toward life. You know, a lot of people are in an arrested stage of development spiritually. They are still teenagers, spiritually speaking. Their attitude is the opposite of that wholehearted trust and glad obedience that says, "I don't understand what's going on, but, hey, I know enough about God that I will follow him. I will put my life in his hands because he has demonstrated thus far who he is and what he does, so I am going to walk with him." That is trust, and only a mature God-follower can exercise it.

However, there is an important difference between doubt and question. A doubting person says, "I don't believe what you say; you'll have to prove it, and prove it on my terms." That is what the Israelites were doing. They were saying in their hearts, "We don't believe God loves us. We don't believe that God brought us out here to take care of us and give us a wonderful heritage. We won't believe it unless God gives us what we want right now." That is doubt.

A questioning person says, on the other hand, "Lord, I know you love me and care about me. Would you show me how you love me? Would you reveal where your love has been shown in my life? Would you show me the evidence of your love?" God loves to prove himself in that way. This is why the psalmist says, "Oh, taste and see that the LORD is good" (Ps 34:8 NKJV). This is what Malachi was talking about when he challenged the people to test God by giving him their full tithe (Mal 3:10). But God hates to be tested by the doubter who says, "I don't believe you, and I won't obey you until you show me on my terms how you are going to do this." To this God says, "You will wait a long time for that proof!"

The two different attitudes also show up when God does demonstrate his care. A questioner is delighted and receives the evidence with delight. A doubter continues to be skeptical and finds plenty of reason to explain away whatever may have happened. So the Hebrew people were coming with the attitude of doubt. They said, in effect, "We don't believe God cares for us, and we won't believe until it is proven to our satisfaction."

Superficially, their murmuring was against Moses. So Exodus 15:23; 16:2; and 17:3 say, "The people murmured against Moses." I believe this indicates that they did not have the kind of intimate relationship with God that would allow them to go directly to him with their cares, so they grumbled at God's man instead. How often that happens, even in the church. We take the pastor apart because we are afraid to take God apart, but, in fact, the one we really doubt is God. Moses makes this very clear in Exodus 16:8, "Moses said, "This shall be seen when the LORD gives you meat to eat in the evening, and in the morning bread to the full; for the LORD hears your complaints [murmurings] which you make against Him. And what are we? Your complaints [murmurings] are not against us but against the LORD" (NKJV). So their murmuring revealed, first of all, that they did not really know God.

In addition, they murmured because of their desire for instant blessing. They wanted their needs met in their way and they wanted it now. How much more common is that tendency in our instant age! "Lord, I got into this relationship with you so you would bless me. You haven't blessed me yet, so you have thirty-seven seconds left to do it." God will respond, "Then it will be at least thirty-eight seconds until I do it." God does not honor a lust for blessing.

Some expect God to bless them in quid pro quo fashion. They say, "Now Lord, I'll serve you as long as you bless me. I'll serve you as long as you supply my needs. I'll serve you as long as you do things my way. So come on. Give me, give me, produce, produce." But God responds, "That is not why I delivered you from bondage. I didn't save you to bless you; I saved you that you might know me, the one who is blessing."

Since the Israelites did not really know God and wanted his instant blessing, they were constantly looking back at Egypt. We see it over and over again in these chapters. "Oh, remember good old Egypt? Remember all the radishes and garlic we used to have back there? Now all we've got is this bland manna. My, we had all the water we wanted to drink. And think of all the wonderful plants..." What about the chains, the whips, and the curses of their oppressors? What about the struggle and strain of Egypt? Their memory was highly selective.

Selective memory is not necessarily a bad thing, of course. I am glad that my memory has a way of blocking out some sad things from my past. I can look back on something that my mind tells me was very painful and troublesome, and yet after all these years the actual pain of it is gone. That is good, and I am glad for it. By the same token, selective memory betrays us if it allows us to look back at days of evil and tragedy and forget what really happened. The Hebrews' memory did that: Upset about their present conditions, they glorified a past that had actually been anything but glorious. How different it would have been if they could have said, "We'll trust God for what he is going to do today. We'll trust God for his creative new way of approaching today's problems. We'll not try to put God in the box of the past. We will trust you, Lord, to do a new thing with us."

Are you tempted to murmur? I am. To all of us, Yahweh says, "Forget the past, forget your desire for blessing, and let me show you today who I am and how much I care for you." Will you let him do that?

### The Provision of Water (15:22–27; 17:1–7)

Over against the people's difficulty with trust in the wilderness, we see God's provision. He provides water twice, and both instances teach significant lessons. The first time, he turns bitter water into sweet. That is what our God can do. He can take the bitterest experiences of life and transform them into something good, worthwhile, useful, and sweet.

Undoubtedly, while many of the Hebrews were sugar-coating their Egyptian experience, the bitterness of that experience was still all too real for many others. Perhaps they remembered a son beaten to death or a daughter dragged off into sexual slavery. But here, where the waters of bitterness were turned sweet, God was whispering to them, "Give me the bitterness of your life; I can take the sting out of it."

You may say, "Oh, John, you don't know the bitterness in which I am living now—the bitterness of a broken marriage, of a wayward child, of hopes turned sour. You don't know." That is certainly true, but I do know God, and God knows the tree that can be thrown into the bitterest waters and turn them sweet.

Scripture does not tell us what kind of tree Moses threw into the water at Marah, and I do not think that it makes a great deal of difference. Neither do I know whether the Holy Spirit specifically intended that miracle to point to the cross when it was given. However, I am confident that the similarity between the tree at Marah and the tree on which Jesus hung is not merely coincidental. A consistency runs through the Scriptures from end to end. Yahweh is the same God from Genesis to Revelation, and what he does in one place is always fundamentally consistent with what he does elsewhere. Everything he does is ultimately bound up in the cross. Whatever Yahweh does in Scripture finds its fullness in the cross.

So what God did at the bitter spring of Marah finds its fullest expression in the cross. The cross can turn the bitterest water in your life into sweet water, if you will allow God to do it. Allow

God to take that cross of your present bitter experience and pour the blood of Christ over it. He can change it from bitter to sweet. Surrender your bitterness, your grief, your pain, and cling to Christ's cross. By that cross, God takes all the bitterness of all the world into himself and transforms it, if we will let him, into sweet water.

The second experience of water (17:1–7) is also extremely instructive. It begins again with the people complaining and grumbling, even to the point of slandering Moses. ("You brought us out here to kill us, didn't you, Moses?") Think of spending forty years trying to lead a people like that. Some of us in the ministry are clamoring for a different assignment within a year or two. Not Moses; he persevered. It is true that at one point (Num 11:15) he asked God to kill him on the spot and get it over with, but that was rare.

In this case, God does not say, "Now look, Moses, you go find a bitter water hole and then I will show you a tree that you can throw into the bitter water hole and turn it sweet." He does not tell the Israelites merely to repeat what they had done the last time. Rather he has something new for them. That is the way of our God, the Creator. Why should he do the same thing twice? We want him to act the same in every situation so we can put him into a box of perfect predictability; then we could control him more easily. But that is not going to happen. Yahweh's character is absolutely consistent, but his actions are not predictable.

Here God pointed out a particular rock and said that if Moses would strike it with his rod, water would pour out of it. Why a rock? Surely that is the last place one would go to find water. Even in soil there is a certain water content, and perhaps a geophysicist could demonstrate that there are traces of water in rock too. But our common sense would say that the thing that has the least water in it would be a rock. Yet God says, "Go to the rock." Moses could have answered, "God, that is hopeless. There is no water in a rock." Fortunately for us all, he did not. He struck the rock and water gushed forth.

What was God saying in this miracle? Out of the hardest, most obdurate, most hopeless situations, he can accomplish his good purposes. The only question is whether we, like Moses, will dare to believe God's promises and will bring our hopeless, impossible rocks to him in faith.

However, there is another side to the imagery of the rock. Throughout the Bible, God is referred to as the Rock. This implies that God is our defense. If you were being chased by enemies and could get on top of a great rock, you could hold them off until help could reach you. So God is a rock of defense. The rock image also implies a cool, sheltering shade. If you are out in an arid wilderness in the Middle East in the summer, you need something to protect you from the pitiless heat of the sun. If you can find a big rock jutting up out of the earth, you can rest in its shadow and find respite from the heat. The same would be true in a storm of wind. We can take shelter in the shadow of a rock.

This passage reveals God, our Rock, in another light. Yes, he is our defense and shelter from the heat and the storms of life, but he is also the rock out of whom flows a spring of living water for his people. Are you drinking at his stream? How easily we forget where our resources are! We forget that refreshment comes, not from ourselves, but from God. So day after day, we try to "work it up" and "keep it going," trying to keep the freshness in our lives. Yet God says, "Child, won't you learn? The water is a gift from the Rock. Draw refreshment from me."

*Provision of Food (16:1–36)*

Not only did God provide water in the wilderness, but he provided food. Every child in Sunday school knows the story of the manna. The name of this substance reminds us that God has a sense of humor. According to Exodus 16:15, when the Hebrews saw the white material on the ground, they did not know what it was, so they said, *"mân hû'?"* which means, "What is it?" So God said they could call it *mân* (what?) for the next forty years. Oh, how often we respond to God's blessings that way! We have figured out a way God could meet our needs, and when he does it in an altogether different way, we say, "What is it?"

We find many lessons in this passage, most of them clustered around the idea of hoarding. God said the Israelites were to gather just as much food as they needed for their families, neither more nor less. Even without reading the account, you can guess what happened next. People went rushing out and began filling every container they could lay their hands on. But when they finally got back to the camp, everyone had just what they needed and no more, and a lot of them had empty bushel baskets that had been full.

God said two other things. On Friday, they were to gather twice as much, because there would be no food on Saturday. Further, they were to eat everything they gathered each day because it would not keep till morning. But did the people believe God in these things? Some did, but many did not. They hoarded what they could because there might not be any tomorrow, and they wanted to save some for the morning. But when they got up in the morning, the stuff they had saved stank. It was rotten, while there was more food—fresh, clean, and pure—on the ground, provided by God. Likewise, some people did not collect enough on Friday and went out on Saturday morning to get some but found the ground bare. God says, "I will provide your needs, but no more than you need."

Why do we hoard things? Why do we clutch things to ourselves? I know that original sin runs deep in the Oswalt family. I learned that when we had children. If you give two little boys two identical trucks and you put them on the floor with their trucks and you look at them, what will you see? You will see each of them looking at the other truck with lust written all over his innocent little face. "I want that one *and* this one."

You see it in our adult scramblings. Two of us live in a huge house and say, "My house isn't so big. All I've got is four bedrooms." So what do you do? Rotate bedrooms every night? As far as I know, you can only sleep in one bed at one time. What is this hoarding instinct about us? I believe it stems from our fearfulness. We are afraid we won't have enough, afraid that we can't depend on God in the moment of need.

Sadly, hoarding is also due to our lust. We usually limit the concept of lust to sexual desire, but it applies equally to all the desires. Lust is the sense that if a little is good, a lot would be better. That is where alcoholism, drug addiction, and every other addiction comes from. It is that conviction that if one pleasant feeling is good, five hundred pleasant feelings would be better, so we are driven on and on and on, to acquire more and more. So here it is with the manna: "My, that manna is very satisfying. Two tablespoons were really good, and it leaves me feeling pleasantly full. Wouldn't ten tablespoons be better?"

The lie the devil tells you is that if you just had all you want, you would be satisfied. The trap is in that word *want*. Need and want are two very different things. This may be why the prohibition of covetousness is the final commandment. In many ways this unbridled wanting is the cause of breaking all the rest of the commands. If want is the controlling factor, then we will never be satisfied, because there is no end to our wanting. Nothing on earth can finally satisfy it.

But the devil tells us another lie, the one he has been telling since the garden of Eden. He tells us that God does not want to give us even what we need, let alone what we want. So what do we say? "I am not going to be dependent on anybody else. I am not going to be dependent on God. I can take care of myself. This manna is here, and I am going to be industrious and diligent and hardworking, and I am going to get it all together and I am going to put it in my box and tomorrow morning I won't have to depend upon God." I am not saying we should not work, nor am I saying we should not be diligent and faithful. But often hard work and diligence just mask proud independence. An industrious person may be thinking, *I can take care of myself and I don't need to depend upon God.*

You may say, "That is not true, I am depending on the Lord," when in fact you are depending on a salary or wage guaranteed in contract. You may be depending on retirement investments, life insurance, or some other security, as if you think you could take care of yourself if God should go on a vacation for six or eight months. We need to hold up a mirror to our faces and ask, "Am I really depending on God day by day?"

For instance, one request in the Lord's Prayer is really rather pointless for most of us. "Give us our food for this day." Why ask for that? Today's meal is at home in the oven, and tomorrow's meal is in the cupboard, along with the next day's and the next and the next. You may be asking, "Wait a minute, Oswalt, what are you saying? We should only shop one day at a time?" No, but I am saying that, particularly in terms of our comfort and daily provision, we should be triply careful as to whether our talk about depending on God is really only hot air. Our fear, our lust, and our pride are constant temptations. God says, "Children, you are not the suppliers of your needs. You can't take care of yourself. You weren't made to take care of yourself. You were made for me to take care of."

I teach at Asbury Theological Seminary, and it seems that almost every year we have some people arrive to go to school who are crazy, to put it bluntly. They have sold everything they have. Their few remaining possessions are in the back of a pickup truck. They are in their thirties, a long time out of college. They have three kids.

"Do you know where you are going to live?"

"Nope."

"Does your wife have a job?"

"Not yet."

"Are you going to get a job?"

"Nope, going to study."

"How much money do you have?"

"Two hundred and fifty dollars."

Crazy. Then comes the unanswerable remark: "But God brought us here."

And do you know what? In case after case, God cares for those crazy people. I am not suggesting that all of us should do that; some of us could not, because the experience would drive us really crazy. Genuine trust does not necessarily require extreme measures. But when those people graduate from seminary, they go out knowing something that their more provident peers don't know. They know that God can be trusted, that he can be depended on. God will take care of you.

That was the point God was trying to convey through the manna. The Israelites could depend on him; they must not depend on themselves to gather and hoard and protect and supply, so that they could say, "Go ahead, God. You can take care of somebody else, I've got mine." God was attempting to teach them that they could depend on him. They could let their weight down on him. He did care for them, and the same power that destroyed the enemy was now dedicated to their care.

### Provision of Protection (17:8–16)

Not only does Yahweh provide food and water, he also provides protection. What is remarkable about this incident is the identity of the people attacking Israel. These were the Amalekites. While we do not know exactly where Mt. Sinai was located, it was surely in the southern part of the Sinai Peninsula. This was not the home territory of the Amalekites; they were from the southern part of Canaan known as the Negev, or south country. This means that the Amalekite warriors traveled some 150 miles in order to attack the Israelites. Since we are not told why they did such a remarkable thing, we can only speculate as to their reasons. Perhaps they heard that the Israelites had brought a lot of booty from Egypt and that they were a poorly organized rabble who would not be prepared to defend themselves. In any case, it was an example of raw aggression whose result, if successful, would be to block the flow of God's love to the world. That is a dangerous place to be. God has called these people because through them he is going to bring the Messiah. God has called these people because through them he is going to manifest his love to the entire world. To all of this, the Amalekites say, "No."

So the battle is joined. This was the Israelites' chance to demonstrate that they are not just slaves but men, and they could make their way in the world. So the battle clashed and roared.

At first, the Israelites did very well. But eventually they began to fall back and some of their best warriors were getting killed. So they said, "What is wrong? What is happening?" Then someone looked at Moses and saw that his hands, which had been raised in blessing, were sagging down. So Aaron and Hur rushed to lift Moses' hands up. Sure enough, the Israelites started winning again and ultimately defeated their enemies. What a strange story. What is it about? Magical actions that enable an army to prevail? No, it is not.

This strange story is an illustration of the truth that would be spoken to Zerubbabel many years later, "'Not by might nor by power, but by My Spirit,' says the LORD" (Zech 4:6 NKJV). God won the battle over the Amalekites. As long as God's blessing was upon them through Moses' raised hands, victory was theirs. There was no miraculous power in Moses' hands. However, the raised staff through which the plagues had come upon Egypt was a symbol of God's presence and protection among them. Even though it took the Israelites more than forty years to learn the lesson, its truth was plain for some to see. It is not your strength, nor is it your power, but it is God's blessing that makes all the difference. If you have that, you have all the power in the universe. To be sure, the Israelites had to fight, but their efforts were only the agency through which the power of God could flow.

### Provision of Organization (18:1–27)

God's final provision was organization. Up to now, God had provided miraculously. But in this case he provided through ordinary means, namely through Moses' father-in-law, Jethro. We are reminded that God has many ways of providing aid to his people, and we should not think less of his provision when it comes through ordinary channels.

Apparently, Moses had sent Zipporah and their two sons back from Egypt to stay with Jethro at some point, perhaps when the conflict with Pharaoh was becoming particularly dangerous. Now Jethro was bringing them to meet Moses. Jethro found that Moses was attempting to administer the entire group of people by himself. Every decision that needed to be made, whether large or small, was brought to Moses. This is not surprising because it seems to be the way Egypt had functioned. Pharaoh was god. So if you wanted to know what god wanted, you got a message to Pharaoh and Pharaoh had to make a decision. To date, no law codes have been found in Egypt. Apparently, every judgment was ad hoc, done on the basis of Pharaoh's most recent decision. This seems to be the way Moses was functioning, acting as though he was Pharaoh.

When Jethro saw what was going on, he said to Moses, "You are going to kill yourself if you go on this way. You don't have to make every decision." He said, "I will give you counsel and God will be with you. It is fine for you to represent the people before God and then relay his statutes and the laws to them. But you must then select reliable and trustworthy leaders of thousands, and hundreds, and fifties, and tens and empower them to apply those statutes and laws to their groups Then you will only have to deal with special cases" (Ex 18:19–22). Through Jethro, God was preparing Moses for the way in which God would govern his people with shared responsibility. This will become clearer in the next chapter.

God is not providing here in a miraculous or a supernatural way, yet this reorganization of the people is still a divine provision through the wise counsel of another human. As I said above, I am very glad that it is a part of this sequence. If all of God's provisions for the people in this part of the book had been miraculous, then we might assume that all of God's provisions in our lives would have to be miraculous as well. But the presence of this provision reminds us to look for his provisions all around us and be thankful. We must never rule out the miraculous; we ought to expect it and we ought to praise God for it when it comes. But at the same time, we must never forget the normal and ordinary ways in which he provides for us every day, and be grateful.

So this part of the book (Ex 15:22–18:27) is a revelation of the caring heart of God. If 1:1–15:21 revealed the power of Yahweh, this section reveals his providence. He knows our most basic needs and cares about them. Clearly many of the people did not get it, as their murmuring shows. But the lesson is there: we can trust our needs to the great I AM. In many ways the whole Pentateuch, the first five books of the Bible, is about this one point: Who supplies our needs? The Enemy told our first parents that they could not trust God to supply them and they would have to do it for themselves. Tragically, they learned that we humans do not even know what our real needs are, much less be able to supply them out of our tiny resources. If you believe you can supply your needs, which is what most of the world believes today, you are sadly deluded. You cannot supply your needs, most particularly your need for fellowship with God.

But if you come to the point where you understand that he can supply your needs better than you can, if you come to the point where you understand that he is dependable and what he supplies is clean, if you come to the point where you can live in gratitude rather than pride, then you have learned the lesson that God is teaching in this part of Exodus, and indeed in the whole Bible.

### Jethro's Faith

Before we leave this section, one more incident deserves our attention. Before Jethro advised Moses about organization, something wonderful had taken place. As soon as Jethro and Moses had done all the conventional aspects of greeting that were expected in that highly structured society, Moses could not restrain himself. He had to tell Jethro the amazing things that had happened to them. "Moses told his father–in–law all that the Lord had done to Pharaoh and to the Egyptians for Israel's sake, all the hardship that had come upon them on the way, and how the Lord had delivered them" (18:8 nkjv). Moses told Jethro about Yahweh's power over the enemy. He told him about Yahweh's providence in need. He told him that the One who is the very source of the universe had come to them with power and love, keeping his ancient promises and showing that the gods are nothing.

This is the first testimony in the Bible, the first witness to someone else about God's work in the world. Jethro's response is thrilling: "'Blessed be Yahweh who has delivered you out of the hand of the Egyptians, out of the hand of the Pharaoh, who has delivered the people from under the hand of the Egyptians.' And then this: 'Now I know [that is, I know for myself] that Yahweh is greater than all the gods, for in everything in which they behave proudly, he was above them.' Then Jethro, Moses' father-in-law, took a burnt offering and sacrifices to God; and Aaron came with all the elders of Israel to eat bread with Moses' father-in-law before God" (18:11–12).

Perhaps you are saying, "What is so exciting about that?" Simply this: Jethro is the first person in the history of the world who got converted because of somebody else's testimony. Jethro had not been there; he had not seen the plagues. Jethro had not been there; he had not seen that rock become a water fountain. Jethro had not been there; he had not seen how God had defeated the Amalekites. But Moses bore witness to what Yahweh had done before their eyes in time and space, and Jethro responded, "On the basis of what you have told me, I know, I know!" Many of the Hebrews who did experience those things seem not to have gotten the point, but Jethro said in an act of faith, "I accept the truth of your testimony, and in the light of that testimony I know that Yahweh alone is God."

Jethro is the prototype of every Christian believer today. Every one of us has been given a testimony of what God has done in time and space, who he has shown himself to be, and we have said, "I accept the truth of that testimony and in the light of that testimony I know that God is the Lord and that Jesus Christ is his Son. I know in light of his cross and the empty tomb that God has forgiven for me of my sins and delivered me to new life. I know, thank God."

If the Bible is just a bunch of fairy tales, made-up stories to express some fuzzy religious belief, we must give up our silly delusions. There is no meaning to life and no hope after death; it is all a horrible joke that the universe has played on us, and the people responsible for the book of Exodus do not know any more about the truth than we do.

But thank God, the Bible is not a collection of fairy tales or fictionalized theology. It is a reliable testimony to what God has done in time and space. It is an account of how God has broken into human history and demonstrated himself. We cannot go up to heaven to find out what he is like, who he is, and what he does. So I AM has come here into our time and space to reveal himself in terms we can understand. Thus, the question for us is: Having heard the testimony, will we accept it?

Jethro did. He said, "Praise God. I know you, Moses. Even though you married my best daughter and took her away from me, I know that you are a man of integrity, I know that what you have told me surely happened, and on that basis I can't do anything else but believe."

Do you know that he is Yahweh? Not merely intellectually but as the basis of your living? When the clouds are dark, when there is nothing in front of you but a brick wall, when the month goes longer than the money, do you know he is Yahweh? When you stand at the open casket of a loved one and think about the empty house that waits for you, do you know he is Yahweh? When you look at a world where evil seems rampant and triumphant, do you know he is Yahweh? Yes, now I know that he is Yahweh, the great I AM.

# Questions for Personal Study or Discussion

1. The Israelites complained about lacking several things as they journeyed through the wilderness. In your opinion, which ones were necessities and which were creature comforts? Which type of need do you most often ask God to supply?

2. What's the difference between doubting God and questioning God? Name several well-known people of the Bible who doubted or questioned God in times of hardship.

3. When people are physically tested, what are some other ways they respond to God? Which kinds of response are most likely to strengthen our faith?

4. Compare the Hebrews' various ways of handling their daily supply of manna (e.g., some hoarded it, others wasted it, and others neglected to harvest it while they could). What are some things we learn from them that would help us be better stewards of our possessions?

5. Reflect on what the Israelites learned in their battle with the Amalekites (Ex 17:8–16). In light of this, what measures do you think you should take to protect yourself from dangerous people?

6. If Jethro were to give you advice about your time management, as he did for Moses, what do you think he would say?

# CHAPTER 8

# The Revelation of Yahweh's Principles
## (19:1–24:18)—Part 1

In our study of the book of Exodus thus far, we have seen that God had much more in mind than merely delivering his people from Egypt. He was bringing them to an understanding of himself, to an understanding of themselves, and to an understanding of what he wants to do in the world. So he not only intended to deliver them from physical bondage, he also intended to deliver them from spiritual darkness and, ultimately, from alienation from himself.

Thus far in the book, we have seen the revelation of Yahweh's power as he defeated the gods of Egypt and the revelation of his providence as he provided the basic needs of the people in the desert. But what about his character, those qualities and principles that express who he is and how he functions? The problem of bondage had been fully addressed—they were free. But the problem of spiritual darkness had only begun to be addressed. If we are to be truly delivered as Yahweh intends, we must know him, who he is and what he is like. In Exodus 19–24, that problem will be addressed in the most thorough ways.

## The Pagan Understanding of Reality

In attempting to address their darkness and reveal his true identity, God was faced with a most difficult problem. Those of us who have grown up in a nominally Christian country, who have grown up in the church, may not sense how severe that problem was. God had to reveal himself in the face of humanly devised religion, which is diametrically opposite to the biblical truth. For four hundred years, the Hebrew people had been immersed in that other kind of religion, that other way of thinking. The Egyptian religion was a perfect expression of it, a religion that the early Christians labeled "paganism." Sometimes we associate paganism with primitive or backward thought, but that is not the half of it. Paganism can be profound and sophisticated. It certainly was in Egypt, and it had surrounded the Israelites on every side; there is no way that they could have avoided coming to think in those ways. Even if they maintained some loyalty to the "God of the Fathers," there is no way they could have escaped the pervasive pagan influence around them (see Josh 24:14).

What were the tenets of this humanly devised religion that shaped Egypt and whose principles continue to guide much of the world today? I want to take the space here to describe them, because in understanding them we will see how radically different reality really is, and what a serious problem Yahweh had to overcome. We will look at the six most important characteristics at the heart of this false religion, which is found in one form or another all over the world: (1) god is the cosmos; the cosmos is god; (2) there is no purpose in existence; (3) there are many gods; (4) there is no single standard of ethics or behavior; (5) divine power is manipulated by manipulating this world; and (6) sex is the elemental life force.

## The Cosmos Is God

Humanly devised religion assumes that the cosmos is all there is; there is nothing beyond it, outside of it, or other than it. In effect, this cosmos is god. So, the earth is god, the sky is god, the wind is god, the trees are god. I am god and you are god. Love is god and sex is god; good is god and evil is god. That is a core conviction of these human religions. God is the world. Take all of the psycho-socio-physical elements in the world, lump them all together and whatever that is, that is god. Actually, if there had been no special revelation of God, this view would make a lot of sense. What else could there be if we do not know anything else? Thus, the first point of humanly devised religion is that this world is ultimate; there is nothing else.

## No Purpose in Life

Humanly devised religion holds that there is no purpose or goal in life. This is obvious if we just look at the world around us. What goal does the thunderstorm have? What goal does the Mississippi River have? What purpose does the grass have in coming up year after year? The answer, of course, is none. These things just happen. If the world is god, then there is no divine purpose for life and no divine plan for daily living. People are born, they live, they die; more people are born and live and die. If there is a purpose of this cycle, it is survival. But survival for what? If the world is god, then there is no purpose in life.

## Many Gods

If this cosmos is god, then it is obvious that diversity, not unity, is the main principle. Deity is diverse just as the cosmos is. There must be a moon god, a sun god, a god of the forest, another of the river, and still another of the stars. The ancient Greek philosophers, brilliant men all, tried to discover some common force or element that unified the cosmos, but they could not; the incredible diversity and complexity of the world defeated them. If the cosmos is all there is, and the cosmos is full of diversity, then the divinity of the cosmos must be expressed in many, many gods.

## No Single Standard of Ethics

If there are many gods, all competing for power, and if there is no purpose but survival, then there cannot possibly be a single standard of behavior. The orange god says, "If you wear green, I'll get you." The green god says, "If you wear orange, I'll get you." So what do you do? You wear a lot of brown and try to keep a low profile. Survive as long as you can with tooth and claw, and when the death angel comes, fight him like a demon. Otherwise you can resign yourself to his grip. You know that in either case you are going to lose. Why then should we observe any standard of ethics? If the world is god, you can do your thing and I can do my thing, and no one can tell me that my thing is wrong. We all just do what works for us and call it right.

## Divine Power Manipulated by Magic

Divine power can be manipulated by manipulating this world. If you want god to do something for you, there are ways to force his hand. You ensure that the links between the visible and the invisible realms are intact by speaking certain words or performing certain actions that have proven effective in the past, and then you manipulate some visible element in a prescribed way. Unless the demons have disturbed the linkage, you get what you want. This is what the Bible calls sorcery. In the Western world, we also know it as voodoo and other forms of the occult. You figure out how to do something here in the visible world that changes the status quo of the invisible world. For example, if you want someone to have a stomachache, you make a little statue and you write that person's name on it. And if you really want this charm to work, follow the person around to get a fingernail clipping, or perhaps a strand of hair, and stick it on that little statue. Then you say some magical words and stab the statue in the stomach with a hat pin. If you did everything right, your victim will get a stomachache.

Humanly devised religion holds that these same principles work on the divine level. You can make the powers obey you if you know how to do it, if you know how to manipulate this world. This is where idolatry comes from. How do I make the storm god do what I want? I make a human-shaped statue of Baal, the lord of power and the lord of the storm. Then I put a very nice suit of clothes on him and say something like this, "Do you like that suit, Baal? Well, let me tell you something, if doesn't rain tomorrow, you are going to go naked." Or perhaps I say to him, "Baal, you like three square meals a day, don't you? [The gods are simply human beings written large.] Well, I've got the finest food in the world for you, and if you give me the rain when I need it, you are going to eat regularly. But if I don't get that rain, Baal, it's going to be a long, hungry summer for you." These examples are oversimplified, of course, but the principle is clear: if this world is god, I can make the divine powers do what I want by manipulating this world.

### The Life Force Expressed in Sexuality

Humanly devised religion holds that sex is the primary force of life. If you control sexual power, you have your hands on the elemental force in the universe. Perhaps you are saying, "Why would anyone think that?" It is not so difficult. If the world is god, where does life come from in this world? It comes from sex.

So our absorption with sex, sexuality, and everything about it is tied to that deep root of paganism in ourselves. People who follow this system of belief suspect that if they can just control that force, they can control life itself. Why is it that so many people jump from bed to bed to bed? Why is it that we have racks of magazines of nude women and nude men? Why is pornography the largest online business by far? Why do our other urges not have the same kind of power over us? It is because fundamentally, deeply rooted in the paganness of the human heart is the belief (often unconscious) that sexuality is the key to power.

These six principles express the religion of the world in a nutshell, and if it all sounds rather like America today, that is no accident. When people disregard the truth revealed in the Bible, when they reject the idea that there is a god who is beyond everything that we are and know, there is really only one alternative: the humanly devised religion—sometimes labeled solipsism or narcissism—which manifests itself in these characteristics and other related ones. Whether it is among aborigines in the Australian Outback or the cultured intellectual Brahmans of India, this is the common understanding of reality in a world where the Bible has not reached.

## The Biblical Understanding of Reality

So this was God's problem. The Hebrew people instinctively believed what their Egyptian neighbors had taught them to believe, and it was wrong at every point. That is the startling thing about this human religion—you would think we would get some of it right even without the special revelation of Scripture. Yet at every one of these key points, this system of belief is diametrically opposed to the truth. God is not the world; he is other than this world.

For Westerners who have been reared in a culture based upon a biblical view of reality, that is not a great surprise. But if you do not know the Word of God, it is upsetting to think that God is utterly beyond this world. We have never experienced anything beyond this psycho-socio-physical cosmos with our own senses, so how can we possibly know there to be anything beyond it?

But if that misconception is wrong—if indeed the One who made this world is other than this world and he is personal—then he could have made it with a purpose in mind. And that is precisely what the Bible says: "He chose us in Him before the foundation of the world, that we should be holy and without blame before Him in love" (Eph 1:4 NKJV). You and I were not born by accident. We do not live our lives by accident. We do not die in senseless oblivion. God made us that we might live in him and progressively and increasingly know him. So on that final day when someone closes the lid on my coffin, it is not a period but a comma, and I go on into an eternity of knowing him and of sharing his character. That is why God made the world.

If Yahweh transcends everything else that is, there cannot be many gods but only One. There is One alone with whom all human beings have to do and before whom all human beings are accountable.

There is a single standard of human ethics, and it is God's standard. It is the way of acting that corresponds to his transcendent character, purpose, and plan. That means certain types of behavior are always and everywhere wrong, and other behavior that is always and everywhere right. Of course, there are areas of human custom where good people may disagree about the best way biblical principles should apply, but that is the only issue. Right and wrong cannot be changed at will to suit my preferences and wishes.

Dr. Dennis Kinlaw, longtime president of Asbury College (now University) and co-founder of the Francis Asbury Society, tells a story that illustrates this point. Riding on a plane one day, Dr. Kinlaw struck up a conversation with his seatmate and learned that the young man was working on a PhD in sociology. Dr. Kinlaw said, "Is it true that from a sociological point of view there really is no right and wrong?"

The young man said, "Yes, that is correct. We simply study what people do, and if this group of people do this, then it is right for them. And if that group of people say that this is wrong, then it is wrong for them. But we can't say there is such a thing as an overall standard of right or wrong. It is just whatever people do."

They went on talking for a while and Dr. Kinlaw said, "Tell me, why did you get into the field of sociology?"

"Well, you know, I just got to thinking there is so much wrong with the world, and I just wanted to do whatever I could to somehow help to straighten things out."

Dr. Kinlaw didn't say anything. The fellow sat there a few seconds, and then his face began to get red. He said, "You trapped me, didn't you?"

Although we dislike the idea and try to suppress it, deep in the human heart is a voice that says what is universally right and wrong. If the whole world were god, that statement would make no sense at all. But if the world is not god—if god is other than the world and has a consistent plan and purpose for us—then a single standard of ethics, which will at times oppose what feels natural, makes all kinds of sense.

Divine power cannot be manipulated by potions, totems, or lucky charms. We cannot make him do what we want by saying a magic mantra or performing a complex ritual. We cannot make him do what we want by reenacting some sort of mechanistic, formalized practice. The only way we can experience God's power is by his graciously giving it to us in response to our trust in his goodness and gracious kindness. That is frightening. We fearful humans do not like knowing that we are unable to make God do what we want. We do not like a God who asks us to jump into the unknown, promising to catch us. An insistent voice of doubt says, "You don't know that he will. Maybe he will drop you." Oh, the proud, fearful, manipulative human heart that says, "I want to live my way. I will tell God when I want him to pick me up and when to let me go. I'll tell God what I need and what I don't need."

To this God says, "No, you won't, child, because you did not make yourself." Yahweh—the great I AM—cannot be manipulated.

Finally, then, sex is not the source of life. The God of love is the Source of life. The tragedy of our society today is that, instead of making love primary and sex a wonderful God–given way of expressing love, we have now made sex primary. So we say, "I guess if you had sex together, you must love one another." What a tragedy! If we make sex the all-important determinant of intimate relationships, then marital love—the best human paradigm of divine love—is rendered meaningless. But if love is all-important, then sex assumes its proper place as a wonderful symbol of the self-abandonment that genuine love is.

## Use of the Covenant Form to Teach the Truth

So you see God's problem with the Israelites in the wilderness. These people, for four hundred years, have been taught to believe the exact opposite of the truth. How could God set them straight? Should he drop a philosophy book on them? Hardly! They were ex-slaves, the majority of whom had no education at all. Besides, as important as learning knowledge is, that is not the way we learn best.

I remember something one of my Hebrew professors said to me. I had been studying the language for two and half years and some parts of it were still pretty murky to me. So I said to him, "I don't think I am ever going to learn this."

He just looked at me and said, "John, after you have taught it four or five years, it won't be much of a problem."

As it turned out, he was right! There is nothing like the terror of the classroom to make one learn very quickly. And how do we learn? We learn best by doing, by living, and by practicing the great truths of life. And that is exactly what God called his people to do.

Obviously, he could not put his instruction in any of the religious forms of the day. He could not take any of the Egyptian or Canaanite myths and rework them, because they were shot through with all these false ideas. So he used a political form to teach them. He took the form of a treaty, or covenant, between a great king and a subject people, and he used that as the vehicle to reveal who he is and what life is about. What creativity! What daring!

### Features of the Covenant

In these treaty or covenant forms, the king says, "I will be your king. I will protect you. I will care for you. I will give you supplies in an emergency. In return, you will not recognize any other king. As far as you are concerned, I am the only king and you will serve me alone. If I am attacked, you will supply troops; if I need resources, you will give your resources." In short, the people swore absolute loyalty to this king alone.

Furthermore, the king would require these people to behave in certain ways, simply because he is their king. He did not have to justify or rationalize the code of behavior he gave them. They were required to do some things and not to do others, as an expression of their identity as his subjects. Out of this covenant, a relationship developed in which the subject people came to know what the king was like. "The king? Well, he hates this stuff and he loves that stuff. That's just the kind of person he is." Do you see what a wonderful device this is for God's teaching purposes? He is able to reveal his character and nature to them through the terms of the covenant.

*Important Aspects of the*
*Covenant for Teaching God's Character*
There were some aspects of the covenant form that were especially appropriate for conveying some of the things about himself and reality that Yahweh wanted to convey.

**Respect for the importance of history.** Covenants typically began with a brief historical explanation as to why this covenant was being offered. Usually, it was because the great king had violently conquered his subjects. In the case of Israel, however, it was a very different situation. Here Yahweh had graciously delivered his people from the clutches of their oppressors. So their motivation for entering the covenant was gratitude rather than subjugation. What God had done in human history, in this time and space, revealed his character and nature—not something that was constantly recurring in an invisible world of myth.

**Absolute loyalty to a single king.** A covenant insisted on absolute loyalty to one single king. This was tailor-made for teaching the Israelites that God is one Person. Just as a great king could say to a people that, as far as they were concerned, he was the only king, so Yahweh could say to the Israelites that he was the only God. He did not need to go into a lot of philosophy, arguing logically why there are not any other gods, why other gods cannot exist, and so on. He simply said, "For all practical purposes in your daily lives, there is only one God."

How did the Jews become monotheists? First of all, by acting and living as though there is only one God. The covenant commanded it, so the covenant was ideal for teaching this truth.

**God commits himself to human beings.** The covenant was also an ideal vehicle for teaching that God commits himself to human beings. However unbalanced most of the ancient Near Eastern covenants were, there was still the unmistakable fact that the king obligated himself to protect them. What a wonderful device for teaching a fundamental truth about Yahweh!

Have you ever heard of a thunderstorm committing itself to anybody? Have you ever heard of the Mississippi River committing itself to anybody? Have you ever heard of the sun committing itself to anybody? No, the powers in the world in no way give themselves to us. But Yahweh, the transcendent, almighty, eternal God, says to you and me, "Children, I give myself to you. I commit myself to you. I bind myself to you." Why would God do that? Of all the powers in the universe, he above all could compel us to obey him. He would not have to commit himself to us to gain a commitment from us. But he has chosen to do so. He has bound himself to protect and bless us, so the covenant was an ideal device to show us this truth.

**The ethical character of the Creator.** The covenant was also an ideal device to teach the ethical character of the Creator. As I said above, ancient covenants typically made ethical demands on the people. If a people wanted to be in a covenant with a certain king, they had to live in ways he prescribed. Why? Because that king endorsed that kind of behavior. So Yahweh said, "As far as you people are concerned, there is one way to live: my way. This way is expressive of my character, my desires, my hopes, and my plans, so this will be your way to live."

There is only one way to live as Yahweh's subjects, and it is the right way. It is the way we were made to live. It is the way the one God planned for us to live. It is way that leads us to glory.

*Placing a law code within the context of a covenant*
By using a covenant to reveal his character, God accomplished another thing. The center of the covenant form was a section of stipulations or terms. This list laid out things that both parties of the covenant were required to do. In the covenant with Yahweh, the stipulations are what we call the law. We now know that there were a lot of other law codes in the ancient world, most of them older than Moses. When you examine the content of those law codes, you find that many of the same general concepts—sometimes even the same wording—that appear in them also appear in the stipulations of the covenant in the Bible. When these facts were first discovered, many people said, "Oh, well, the biblical commandments were not really revealed; Moses just copied it all from other ancient law codes." While it is not so common today to say that they were directly copied, many scholars still assert that these laws were just a part of the common culture of the ancient Near East.

However, when these commandments are placed in the context of a covenant with the monarch, the dynamic changes. Other Near Eastern law codes are not found within covenants; rather they were typically promulgated by a king to preserve order in his kingdom. People were supposed to act according to these civil laws; if they did not, they could expect heavy penalties. But all this changes when those ideas are put in the context of a covenant with the ruler himself. All of a sudden now, the way you treat one another, the way you treat your oxen, the way you treat your servant, and so on, are not just expected social norms; now they are an expression of your relationship with the covenant giver. With the Israelites, obedience to covenant law expressed their relationship with Yahweh himself.

Now, if I mistreat my servant, I have not just broken some social contract; I have offended God. For the first time in human history, human ethics become an expression of religious commitment. For the first time, how we treat one another becomes a matter of sin and righteousness. For the pagan, how we treat one another has little or nothing to do with what we believe about deity. How we handle property has little or nothing to do with how we relate to deity. As for the environment—well, the pagan may treat it with a degree of awe because it is the body of god, but the idea of caring for it or developing its potential as a trust from God does not enter the picture. By placing all these kinds of expectations in the context of covenant obedience, God says in effect, "How you treat one another is an expression of your covenant with me. And if you violate these things, you have sinned against me."

The basis of ethical behavior is radically changed. It moves from external (a sense of social obligation or royal coercion) to internal. It is no longer a question of whether my needs are more important than yours, or whether I think I can get away with what I am contemplating. The basic question is whether a person who has sworn to do the will of his covenant lord can do such a thing. It does not matter that telling a lie might be to my advantage and that nobody is likely to catch me in it—Yahweh will know! The whole reason for ethical living has changed, and changed radically.

Some skeptical scholars feel this still does not explain why the Law of Moses uses some of the same general concepts and sometimes even the same wording as that found in the law codes of Israel's neighbors. If Israel's covenant is revealed, would not God have used some other language or other ideas?

To the contrary, it would be surprising if God had written certain principles into the very nature of reality and they did not appear anywhere else but in the Bible. Why did the kings make lying and theft criminal offenses? Because no society on earth can long survive when theft and lying are the norm. And why is that, I wonder? Because those things violate the very design of the universe, which reflects the character of the Designer.

So what God is saying when he appropriates some concepts and words from pagan law codes is this: Thoughtful pagans have gotten a glimpse of the truth, and as far as they go, they are right. But these are not just good principles of justice, just something society expects and works better with. No, they are written into the very fabric of the universe. So the way you treat your wife, the way you treat your husband, the way you treat your neighbor are all expressions of who you are in God. By putting those behaviors in the context of covenant, God changed the whole nature of law for the rest of time.

Tragically, Western civilization is now beginning to lose this connection. It is becoming commonplace for people to say, "How I treat you doesn't have any relationship to ultimate value. It is just a good idea for orderly society." It has taken us thirty-five hundred years to drift away from the truth that God gave us when he put his laws, his torah, into the hands of his people. But drift we have.

### The Covenant's Placement and the Nature of Salvation

Finally, there is another very important thing that the covenant shows us, which relates to our understanding of salvation. A wrong theology has grown up in the church, and unfortunately it is especially prominent among modern evangelicals. This is the idea that the law was only given to damn people, to bring them under condemnation, so that they could then be saved by grace. The effect of this is that too many Christians, while they would not say it out loud, really believe that it does not matter how a Christian lives since we were never intended to keep these commandments anyway. Current sociological surveys show no measureable difference between the lifestyles of Christian believers and the lifestyles of the lost. This reflects the pervasive influence of Christian lawlessness with tragic emphasis. An alternative idea is almost as dangerous: This is the idea that God's covenant law was given so the Israelites could be saved, but it does not really apply to non-Israelites, or Gentiles. In either case, it is assumed that the old covenant has no relevance for modern Christians.

Neither idea is correct. To be sure, the Israelites were unable to keep their covenant, but that does not mean it was only given to condemn them. And the Law certainly was not given as the means of their salvation, their reconciliation to God. No, the Old Testament teaches us that we are saved by grace. The apostle Paul emphasized this in the book of Galatians when he argued that Abraham came into a saving relationship with God long before the law was given.

But that was not only true of Abraham. Think with me for a moment: How were the Israelites saved from Egypt? By their obedience? Did God reveal his covenant to them in Egypt, and did they keep it so well that he delivered them? Of course not! If they had had to fulfill the covenant in order to be delivered, they would still be in Egypt!

No, Moses showed up on the scene, and told them to pack their bags. When they asked why, he said, "Because we're leaving."

"Why?" they asked.

"Because God is delivering you."

"Why?"

"Because he loves you."

"Why?"

"Because that's who he is!"

Do you see what I am saying? The exodus from Egypt was by grace. God delivered the people from Egypt by grace alone. They didn't have to do a thing except get up and go.

Now hundreds of miles were behind them. They are camping at the foot of Mount Sinai, and God says, "Would you like to be my people?"

"Of course," they respond, "we saw what you did in Egypt."

"That's good, because I want to be your God. But if you are going to walk with me, you have to be like me."

Do you remember what it was like to fall in love? You wanted to find out everything you could about that person. You wanted to find out what they liked and did not like, what they did and what they did not do. Why was that? Because you wanted to please them, to do things that would make the relationship work. The love was already there, and sometimes you could hardly believe that the other person loved you—but they did! So you wanted to do everything in your power to keep that relationship going.

That is exactly what Sinai was about. The Hebrew people were already in a relationship with God, one that he had initiated in grace. Now he was giving them the means by which that relationship could grow and become strong. The Law in its covenant form was not the *way to* God, it was the *walk with* God. If you are going to walk with God, you have got to be like him. But that walk begins by his grace. The whole Bible teaches this pattern.

Perhaps you are saying, "Now wait a minute, didn't Jesus and Paul condemn any attempt to save yourself by keeping the law? Didn't they say that Jesus came to deliver us from the curse of the law?" Yes, they did. But they were attacking a Pharisaic perversion of the Old Testament, not what the Old Testament itself teaches. Where did this perverted understanding come from? From that fact that we humans hate grace. We like to believe that we only get what we have earned.

You know what I am talking about. Someone does something for you that you absolutely do not deserve. How do you feel? You feel humiliated, and you start thinking in one of two ways: (1) You imagine that maybe you really did deserve that favor after all. Or (2) if you cannot convince yourself of that, you think of ways you can pay the person back. Accepting grace is hard.

It was just like that for the most earnest and faithful Jews of Jesus' day, the Pharisees. They could not believe that the just and holy God of the Old Testament would invite anybody into his arms on the basis of grace alone. So they concluded that he had given his people the law so that really, really obedient people (like them) could earn their way to heaven. To that idea, both Jesus and Paul say a resounding no. They say that if you try to use the law in that way, it will only condemn you, because that is not why it was given.

In the covenant, Yahweh says that if you have been saved, you have been saved unto righteousness. The modern American church has largely lost sight of this truth. We think we have been saved so that we don't have to worry about being righteous anymore. But God has delivered us from the consequences of our sin so that we might walk with him in holiness.

The New Testament teaches this. You were not saved by good works, but "you were saved unto good works" (Eph 2:8–10). "You were saved unto righteousness" (Col 3:5–17). "You were saved unto holiness" (Luke 1:74–75; Heb 12:9–12). Nowhere does the New Testament teach that you can get saved by grace, and then if you really want to be a super Christian, you can also decide to be holy. Over and over again, in a variety of ways, it says that we receive salvation, forgiveness of sin, in order that we might walk with God in holiness.

This is what the Old Testament covenant teaches us as well. If you know your Old Testament, you can never get away with the idea of sinning religion. You know that God delivered the Israelites from Egypt so that he could impart his character to them and teach them to live his life in the world. The fact that the majority of them failed in that task cannot obscure the obvious fact that another majority also recognized the truth of everything I have just said. That is why they used such care to preserve these inspired teachings for the future.

## Preparation for the Covenant (19:1–25)

God's use of the covenant form made it possible to address much of the faulty theology that the Israelites brought with them from Egypt and, at the same time to lay further the foundations for a proper understanding of his salvation. This is what we find in Exodus 19–24: God gives his covenant to the people, and the people accept that covenant relationship. This is a critical moment for God's whole revelatory enterprise. In some ways, he had been leading up to it ever since the garden of Eden. Since Eden, he had been working toward this moment when he could present himself and his plan to his people. But would they accept the covenant? Would they agree to this limitation of their apparent freedom to direct their own lives? Only in that kind of absolute surrender to God and his way could they, or we, learn who he really is and what he wants to do in the world.

Suppose the Israelites said, "Well, God, that is very nice, but there seem to be some hooks in that thing. We would rather keep lots of gods that we can manipulate. We don't know whether we really want to sell ourselves out to one god and one way of right and wrong. We kind of like things the way they are."

What would have happened then? Would God have started all over by selecting another nation to follow him? It is hard to say, but it certainly would have been cataclysmic This explains chapter 19. The entire chapter describes how Moses and Aaron prepared their people to accept the covenant.

One of the tragedies of American society is that our young people are not prepared to enter into a covenant with God. As a theology professor and college administrator, I have had a chance to counsel with a number of earnest young Christians. They say to me, "I really want to trust God and I really want to sell out to God. Why can't I?" So I ask about their home life. You can guess their responses. If they cannot trust their parents, it is not surprising that they cannot trust God. In the same way, if they have grown up in a nominal church where the main message is, "Let's all be nice," it is not surprising that they hesitate to answer a call for total surrender. Part of them sincerely wants to do it, but another part jumps back and says, "What is this?" They have no models; they have no preparation for the critical moment.

So at the foot of Mount Sinai, God took the time and effort to prepare the people to say yes. The preparation was remarkably holistic. There was intellectual preparation (vv 3–9). Then there was preparation of the will, or volitional preparation (vv 10–15). Finally, there is preparation through the senses, or affective preparation (vv 16–20). At every level of their personality, the people were prepared to make a positive response to God's offer of an exclusive covenant.

## Intellectual Preparation

The intellectual preparation first involved memory, so the people were to remember what God had done for them in the past (vv 3–4). He had devastated Egypt for their sake and had "borne them to myself on eagle's wings." Look back across your own life and recall the evidences of God's care and protection and power. Why has he done it? To bring you to himself. That ought to motivate you to trust him for the future.

Then they are invited to consider God's promises for the future (vv 5–6). "Now therefore, if you will indeed obey My voice and keep My covenant, then you shall be a special treasure to Me above all people; for all the earth is Mine. And you shall be to Me a kingdom of priests and a holy nation" (NKJV).

I do not know how God can look at all of his children and say with honesty, to everyone, "You are my special favorite." But he does. He looks at each of us and says, "Ah, you are the special one. You are my special treasure; I will do things with you that I will not do with any other people on the earth. I will make you holy to me, belonging to me only, not for anybody else's use. I will make you a kingdom of priests. You will be the mediators through whom the rest of the world will come to me."

These four verses are especially important in that they define what God's intention was for his people. As his special possession, delivered from the hand of the enemy, the Israelites were to have both a function and a character that was unmistakable. They were not saved to enjoy a privileged status, nor so they could live as they chose. Rather, they were saved so that they could be holy. As exclusive possessions of Yahweh, they could serve him by manifesting his life and character in ways that would draw the world to him. They had evidence of the past and promises for the future: intellectual preparation.

### Volitional Preparation

Then comes preparation of the will. We may know something perfectly well and yet not act appropriately on the knowledge. So Yahweh gives his people a chance to take baby steps, as it were, in holy action. He gives them three things to do: First, they are to wash their clothes (v 11); then they are to set limits around the mountain (vv 12–13); and finally, they are to abstain from sexual relations (v 15). All of these actions were ways of consecrating or sanctifying themselves. In these small ways, they were setting themselves apart to belong completely to the holy God and manifest his life in their behavior.

Consider that first command to wash their clothes. Throughout the Bible, dirt is one of the chief symbols of sin. You cannot serve God with filthy clothes. (Of course, clothes are not the real issue; they symbolize an unworthy life.) Shall we appear before the Lord in the rags of our own self-righteousness (Isa 64:6; Matt 22:11–12)? Shall we appear before him in the rags of our own achievements? God alone can make us clean in his sight. The act of washing one's clothes emphasized that fact.

The second command was to build a fence around the bottom of the mountain. The plain truth is that Yahweh is dangerous to us. We can no more exist in his presence in our sinful state than lint can exist when touched by a flame. Unless God himself provides a cleansing for us—something the covenant was leading to—exposure to him is death. "Build a fence," he says. Accidental contact between a holy God and an unholy human being could prove fatal.

Christ has broken down that fence and we can come into the presence of the Most High in perfect security. But because most contemporary Christians are completely ignorant of the Old Testament, we take this safe entrance as simply our right. We treat the Lord of Glory with habitual casualness, as though he were our good buddy, and then we wonder why our worship produces a lot of excitement but profound shallowness. We can live in the presence of the Holy One only because of the death of the Holy One for us. We need to be still aware of that vast chasm between us, which is now bridged by the cross.

The final command is almost a "throwaway" at the end of verse 15. "Oh, by the way, abstain from sex." It is almost as if Yahweh does not want to make too much of this, not give it more prominence than it deserves, but why is it prohibited at all? Is it because sex is evil? No, but it is like dirt: there is nothing inherently evil about it, but it can represent some attitudes contrary to the truth of God. (You cannot read the Song of Solomon and believe that sex is something God does not approve of.)

No, the Israelites were to abstain from sex temporarily for two reasons. The first we have already mentioned: Pagans believed that sexual activity was an important way to participate in the life force of the cosmos and, through it, to manipulate that life force. But God says that we cannot participate in his life, much less manipulate it, through our sexuality. Sex is an aspect of creation, not an aspect of God.

The second reason for this abstinence was the human attitude of self-sufficiency that sex can represent. We are tempted to think we can produce life through our own activity. We can beget sons and daughters who will carry on our lives after us, who will till our fields, who will make us wealthy and comfortable old men or honored, fruitful old women. But our ability, whether sexual or otherwise, cannot save us. Our biological ability to reproduce ourselves through sex is not the source of life. Life is a gift from God, so he wants us to remember that he supplies it.

### Affective Preparation

With these acts of intellectual and volitional preparation complete, we come to the final phase of preparation, the affective. Exodus 19:16–20 is particularly precious to me. When I was a sophomore in college, I came to the place of full surrender to God. Ever since I was thirteen, I had been fighting against God's call to preach. I had come to Taylor University not really knowing what I would do with my life, only what I would not do. But through my freshman year and then into the fall of my sophomore year, the gentle pressure of God became stronger and stronger. In the fall campus revival series, I came to something of an all-or-nothing moment, so I gave my life to him without any reservation, to do whatever he wanted. I am so glad I did.

As a result of that experience, I began to read the Bible systematically for the first time in my life. I figured that if a person were going to read a book, he might as well begin at the beginning. So I started with Genesis 1, and by the following spring I had worked my way through Genesis and into Exodus. I was living in a dorm where there was really only one place to have devotions early in the morning, a little basement laundry room. I need hardly tell you it was no gothic cathedral. The paint was peeling off the wall, it was damp and humid, and every once in a while you would get hit on the head by a drop of water off the steam pipes.

But one morning I came to Exodus 19, and all I can say to you is, I heard the trumpets! I saw the smoke coming down upon the mountain. I felt my soul being lifted up like those Hebrews must have been lifted off their feet by the thunder and lightning. God was there. I would not trade those moments for anything in the world, nothing in the world.

God had prepared the Israelites through their minds, through their actions, and now through their senses. The trumpet blew, the fire fell, the smoke rolled, and the earth trembled. They knew they were in the presence of God; they saw, heard, and felt all the evidence they needed. If there was any way under heaven that they could be moved to accept this awesome covenant, it had been done. The moment had come.

# Questions for Personal Study or Discussion

1.  Dr. Oswalt lists six beliefs (bottom of p. 146, top of p. 147) at the heart of the false religion that influenced the Israelites in Egypt. Beside each one, write the opposite statement. How well do the opposites state the core of faith in the true God? Would you add any statements to these?

2.  Do you agree or disagree with the statement, "There is a single standard of human ethics and it is God's standard"? Why or why not?

3.  Identify several "areas of human custom where good people may disagree about the best way biblical principles should apply." If you disagree with others in your congregation about some of these issues, how do you maintain unity with them?

4.  List several ways that marital love is "the best human paradigm of divine love."

5.  Now list some ways that a single person can reflect divine love—especially any ways that a single person can reflect better, without the obligations of marriage.

6.  God's covenant radically changed the basis for our ethics: It moved from external motivation (a sense of moral duty or royal coercion) to internal motivation (to please God, who sees and knows our intent). Read Jeremiah 9:3–16 and underline phrases that show God judges us according to our intent, even if others think well of us.

7.  Dr. Oswalt says, "If you know your Old Testament, you can never get away with the idea of sinning religion." Examine your behavior in light of this statement. If you are trying to live a kind of "sinning religion," confess and repent of it.

CHAPTER 9

# Revelation of Yahweh's Principles —Part 2

## Presentation of the Covenant (20:1–23:33)

With the careful preparations of chapter 19 complete, we are ready to launch into the actual presentation of the covenant. In the ancient world, the typical covenant form began with an introduction of the speaker and then moved to the historical prologue. This was followed by the stipulations, or terms, of the agreement, and finally the provisions for sealing the covenant. The covenant was sealed by calling on the various gods to witness the blessings that would come to those who kept the covenant and curses upon those who broke it. Exodus chapters 20 through 24 follow this pattern. The introduction of the speaker is found in 20:1; the historical prologue appears in 20:2; and the stipulations for the people follow in 20:3–23:19. These are followed by the commitments of Yahweh in 23:20–33 and then the sealing of the covenant in chapter 24. There we will see a necessary variation in the matter of witnesses.

The stipulations of the Sinai covenant are given in two forms: a brief form (where the stipulations are stated in the form of absolute principles) and a longer form (where concrete examples are given to show how these principles work out in real-life situations). In this chapter, we will look at the introduction, the historical prologue, and the basic principles, which we know as the Ten Commandments. In the following chapter, we will look at the examples and the sealing ceremony.

*Introduction and Historical Prologue*

As mentioned above, the introduction of the speaker appears in Exodus 20:1, where we are told, "And God spoke all these words" (NKJV). Neither Moses nor Aaron nor any other human leader proclaimed this covenant, but God did. If these words are not from God, they are not worth very much; and unless God spoke them, it is hard to explain where they came from. If all the rest of the world says, "God is this, this, and this," and this book alone says, "No, God is these opposite things," how do you explain that? The biblical writers respond, "Oh, it is very simple. God told us." That is good enough for me.

Following the introduction of the speaker comes the historical prologue (20:2). Who is this great king who is offering this covenant, and why should we bind ourselves to him? As we noted earlier, here is a significant difference from most of the political covenants, which were based on coercion. In most cases, a king had defeated the people in war, so they could either continue to oppose him and be destroyed, or accept the terms of his covenant. What a great difference here! "I am the Lord your God, who brought you out of the land of Egypt, out of the house of bondage." This king has graciously delivered his people from bondage, not created a contract of bondage. Accepting his covenant is not a matter of coercion, but of gratitude.

This idea—that obedience is an expression of gratitude—is absolutely vital to our Christian theology of salvation. The law was not given so that the Hebrew people could work their way into a saved relationship with God. Never! They were already in such a relationship because of his gracious deliverance, which had already been accomplished. So what is the proper response to God's gracious salvation? The idea that one can be saved and live in disobedience is simply unthinkable from a biblical perspective. If we try to do that, we really do not understand the incredible thing Christ has done for us in "transferring us from the kingdom of darkness into the kingdom of light" (Col 1:13). Oh, how easily we misunderstand this! Many sincere Christians believe they have come to Christ for salvation, for forgiveness of sin and deliverance from guilt, without understanding that the necessary outcome of deliverance is our commitment to belong to him without a rival and without limit. Why do we hang back from that commitment? Because we do not really understand whose we are and what he did when he saved us. If that fact gets hold of us—that he gave his life for us, that we are living as people who were dead and are now alive, that we owe him everything—then giving ourselves to him in a life completely conformed to his will not be such a tough problem.

### The Stipulations of the Covenant (20:3–23:33)

From the historical prologue we move to the stipulations. As I just said, they are given in two forms: a short one and a longer one. The short form is what we know as the Ten Commandments (20:3–17). These commandments are stated as absolutes, unlike the law codes of the ancient world. Those civil law codes were stated in the form of cases. That is, "If such and such a thing should happen, then this is what should be done." They gave people no unchanging principles, but simply pragmatic (and changeable) ways of addressing specific social problems. In royal covenants, however, kings could say, "You shall not…," or "You shall…" That is, in our covenant relationship, this is the way it will be. Certain unchanging principles will govern our relationship. Once again, this covenant relationship was ideal for what God was seeking to reveal about himself. As the King of the entire universe, he can define what the unchanging principles of behavior are. In his case, these are not merely absolute principles defining the limited relationships between a human conqueror and a subject people. Rather, they are the absolute principles defining the eternal relationships between the Creator and his creatures. The fuller statement of the covenant stipulations (21:1–23:19) takes the form of case law, but placing the ten commandments before them changes the significance of those cases radically. Now they are not merely pragmatic civil laws but the outworking of unchanging principles in the crucible of life.

**Unchanging Principles (Ex 20:3–17).** So what are these unchanging principles? The first four address our relationship with God. They speak of his oneness, his transcendence, his holiness, and the sanctity of time. The remainder speak about our relationships with others, our neighbors, to use New Testament terms. On the surface of it, this proportion is rather strange. After all, this is a covenant with God. Should not all of the stipulations in a covenant with God be about serving God? No, because the purpose of the covenant is not merely to establish the parameters of our relationship with God but also to teach us the character of God. So those last six commandments teach us how God values people and how we must value them as well if we are to live in covenant with him.

The first commandment establishes the remarkable fact that there is only one God. As we noted earlier, this command is stated in a remarkable way. God does not bring forward a complex philosophical argument to convince his people to worship him alone. All he says is, "If you are going to be mine, you cannot recognize any other god." That is what God asks from you and me. That is the foundation of it all. No thing, no person, no concept, no dream, no power, nothing will be god in my life but Yahweh. He does not care what you understand about monotheism or religious philosophy or theology in general. What he cares about is this: Do you have any other gods in your life? Does anything else have equal claim on you? If so, then whatever your philosophy, you are not mine.

The second commandment is like the first in that it is deceptively simple. God says that if the Hebrews are going to be in a covenant with him, they cannot make an image of him. Why is that so important? Because the instant you make God in the shape of anything in the cosmos, you drag him into this world, and when you do that, you are headed straight down the road to paganism. The instant you say, "I have got to visualize him. I have got to fix him into a form my mind can comprehend so that I can relate to him," God says, "You dare not." All of the points of false, humanly devised religion flow from one polluted spring: God is this world. The moment we put God into any of the shapes of this world, we are on the road to saying he is this world.

I think this is why we do not have one physical description of Jesus in the Gospels. We do not know whether he was tall or short, fat or thin, handsome or ugly, dark or light. We do not know the color of his eyes, the shape of his face, or any specific thing about his appearance. I do not mean to say that we should never try to picture Christ; we would have to destroy most of the great art of the world if we did that. But we dare not say, "This is the genuine image of Christ," and begin to pray to it or think of him in those terms. No. God says, "No images."

We are so familiar with these first two commandments that it is easy to forget how revolutionary they are. Think about this for a minute: How many monotheistic religions are there in the world? Just three: Christianity, Judaism, and Islam. Now how many religions absolutely prohibit idols? The answer is: the same three. So where did those three religions get their monotheism and their iconoclasm? All three got it from the same source: the Old Testament. One more question: Where did the Old Testament get these ideas?

If the Old Testament stands alone in the world, with concepts that are in direct contradiction to the central concepts that all the other world religions share, is it reasonable to think that it is just another human attempt to find God? It certainly is not. A much more likely explanation is the one the Israelites give us: We did not dream up these ideas; they were given to us by God himself.

The third commandment has become a bit trivialized in its current usage. For most people, it has come to mean that we should not swear and curse. That is not incorrect, but the meaning of the command goes much farther than that. Its true meaning is linked to the way *name* is used in the Bible. For us moderns, that word primarily denotes a label. So we think that the command is talking about how we use the specific names for God, such as *God* or *Jesus*. But in the Bible, one's name is really one's character or nature. So how do we make God's nature empty (i.e., "in vain")? One way, of course, is to use his label in a casual oath where it has little if any significance. But there are more serious ways to drag God's name in the mud, as it were.

For God to be holy, we must hold him to be high and exalted, unlike any other. So whenever we make God appear little and insignificant, we have emptied his nature and character of its true meaning. When I give him the leftovers of my time, talents, and income, I have taken his name in vain. When I give him one hour of my week and say, "My, aren't I religious?" I have treated him as being unimportant. When I live my daily life without any reference to him, without any evidence of him, I have broken the third commandment. God says, "Make my name and my honor and my glory the most important thing in your life." What he is telling us in this command is to make him truly holy in our lives and behavior, to demonstrate that there is none like him.

That is what happened with David when he came into the Israelite camp and discovered his brothers sitting there while the Philistine giant mocked them and their God. Though he was just a boy, he could not let that man "defy the armies of the Living God" (1 Sam. 17:26). Do we Christians care that much about the name, the honor, the glory, the reputation of Yahweh—or is he just a useful adjunct to our lives? Does he exist to serve us, to accomplish our desires, to answer our prayers, to be a "rabbit's foot" to get us to heaven? Or have we met the God who is so overwhelming, so astonishing, so glorious, so righteous, so true, that our activities never escape the scrutiny of him, his service, and his glory? That is to make him holy, to hallow his name, as we ask every time we pray the Lord's Prayer.

In the first three commandments, Yahweh has established that he is one, that he is not this world, and that he is to be kept holy. Finally, he says that on one day out of every seven, no ordinary work is to be done. What is the point of that? In some ways, this commandment gives practical expression to the first three. Sometimes people say to me, "Keeping the Sabbath is just one of the Jewish ceremonial laws. We don't worry about eating or not eating pork anymore; we don't worry about writing little pieces of the law on the back of our hands anymore. We don't do all those other ceremonial things, and the Sabbath is just one of the ceremonial laws, so it doesn't apply to us." That is not correct. The Sabbath is not just a ceremonial commandment. By putting it in the Ten Commandments, God placed it on a different level from all the rest. If it is merely a ceremonial law, why is it the only one here? Why does he say nothing in the Ten Commandments about sacrifices, holy feasts and fasts, or clean and unclean food? Surely, it is because this command is not just a ceremonial law.

I think God is saying two things with this commandment:

1. "Your time is mine. It is not yours to use as you wish for your purposes, your goals, and your aims." So every seven days, we pull up short and say, "Every day is a gift from God. Every day is a blessing from him. So today, I will stop and remind myself that all my time is the Lord's." If we never do that—if we make the seventh day just like every other day—then we are saying that all time is really ours to use for our pleasure, purposes, and business. When we do that, something significant happens in our relationship with God. The ceiling closes in and we find ourselves living in a little world struggling and striving to do our thing, to make it all come together, to hold it all together, and constantly failing. But if every seven days we open up the ceiling and say, "O Lord, thank you. Thank you for reminding me. It is all yours. Every day is a gift from you. Thank you." Then we remember that keeping our world together is not our responsibility, but his. What freedom, what peace, what a lifting of the burden!

2. The Sabbath teaches me that Yahweh supplies my needs, not I. What are we saying when we insist that we have to work every day of the week to supply our needs? We are saying that we are the source of supply for our lives. That is a lie, of course. I will never forget an experience of my teenage years that brought this home to me. I grew up on a farm. My father was a Christian

believer, although he was not particularly demonstrative in his faith. One summer day, he taught me something about the Sabbath that has been unforgettable. We did not own a hay-baler, so we depended on our neighbor to come and bale our hay. On a particular Saturday, our hay was all raked and dry and ready for the baler. Our neighbor was supposed to come but didn't. Sunday turned out to be a beautiful clear day, and it was supposed to rain on Monday. So when we got home from church that Sunday, I asked Dad if he was going to call the neighbor to have him come over and bale the hay. He looked at me as if I was from another planet. Slowly, he said, "We don't need the hay that bad." Well, we did need it. But we did not need it badly enough to compromise this basic truth of the universe: God supplies our needs, not us, and any time we do something that makes us forget that truth, we do ourselves great harm.

This does not mean we have to become legalists like the Pharisees of Jesus' day, who would not carry something in their pockets on the Sabbath day because that might mean they were carrying a load. It simply means that we refuse to make this day like every other day. We do things on the Sabbath that remind us that all our time is a gift from God and that he, not we, is the supplier of our needs.

Someone may say, "You are very rigorous about making one day different from all the rest, but you really don't keep the Sabbath commandment because you stop your regular activities on the first day of the week, not the seventh." That is because we are Christians, not Jews. We read the whole Bible, not just the first three-quarters. The Old Testament points to Christ. Again and again, a basic principle is established in the practices of the Old Testament and then it is affirmed but transformed in the New Testament. So the Old Testament sacrificial system teaches us that there is no forgiveness of sin without the shedding of blood; the New Testament affirms that principle but shows us that it is only the blood of God himself that can cover our sins. Thus, animal sacrifices are no longer necessary.

It is the same with the Sabbath day. In the Old Testament, the basic principle is established on the seventh day, which celebrates the completion of creation. But creation has become marred by sin, and its perfection is no longer perfect. The good news is that Christ has come to redeem creation, to restore it to all that it was intended to be and even more. So the Christian affirms the fundamental truths of the Sabbath in a celebration of the redemption of creation. We do that at the beginning of the week because on that day the Lord Jesus rose to new life for himself, for us, and for all creation, and on that day the Spirit of God came to live that new life in all of us.

God said to his people, "If you want to honor me, live in relationship to me, and express your gratitude for my delivering you from Egypt, then I ask these four things of you: Recognize no other gods but me. Do not confuse me with this world in any way. Reverence me in everything you do. And remember who gives you time and supplies your needs." Only four things—but they are four very big things.

Then he said that people who are in covenant with him will treat other people in certain ways. Here we see the teaching function of the covenant. As the Israelites sought to live by these commandments, they learned some profound things about the character of Yahweh himself. In many ways, this is where the reality of one's commitment gets tested. If we can just stay in our prayer closets, we can be very holy. But when we have to rub shoulders with one another, when your interests and my interests, when your point of view and my point of view, begin to butt heads with one another, that is when we find out whether we really know God or not.

God says, "Yes, how you treat me is an indication of your character and your relationship to me. But how you treat other people is equally important." This latter area may be even more important, because there are six commands here as opposed to four in the first section.

The first command relating to others is profoundly important because in some ways it sets the stage for the rest: "Honor your father and your mother." What does that mean? It means you will recognize that everything you have and are is a gift, even if your parents are, from some point of view, unworthy of honor. When you keep this command, you are saying, "Father, Mother, thank you for bringing me into this world. Thank you for giving me care when I was helpless. Thank you for myself." Your words and actions to this effect are really saying, "I am not self-created."

Why is that so important? Because if you and I go through life blaming somebody else for who we are and what has become of us, we are never going to be free. Until I am able to say, "This is me. Mom, Dad, thank you," I am not really free. How many young people I meet who are in bondage to their inability to forgive their parents. Bondage. All their days, they think, *If I had just been born to somebody else.* All their days, they think, *If Dad just hadn't been that kind of a man. If Mother just hadn't been that kind of a woman.* What a freeing hour it is when I can say, "Mom, Dad, I know you are not God, and I don't blame you for not being God. I will let you be a fallible man and woman who did the best you could under those circumstances, and I thank you." Then bad memories of our parents no longer hold us in bondage, and we no longer hold them in bondage.

In other words, God says, "If you are going to live with me, let a well of gratitude flow from you. And gratitude has to begin at home." Why is gratitude and praise so hard for some of us? Because we refuse to give it at the most simple, ordinary place—home. If I cannot honor my earthly dad, how can I honor my heavenly Father?

The second covenant principle relating to our attitude toward others is, "Don't murder." It is important to get the language right here. The King James Version says, "Don't kill," but the Hebrew word specifically means murder—one person lying in wait for another in order to take their life. So this commandment does not speak directly to such questions as capital punishment or the permissibility of war. It will be a factor in those discussions, but it does not in itself answer them. The commandment says that I must value the physical lives of others. I cannot use their lives as I wish to satisfy my anger, my hatred, or my greed. God says to each of us, "Their lives are not yours. Each person's life is precious and is a gift from me; it is not yours to extinguish at will. You shall not murder."

"You shall not commit adultery." As with the rest of these principles, this one sums up many other truths. By singling out adultery, God is not suggesting that other sexual offenses are of no interest to him. Instead, he identifies this one offense to indicate his regard for all of them. So this commandment implies that God also forbids premarital sex, bestiality, incest, and homosexual behavior. The prohibition of adultery sums up all the rest. Why would he do that?

For most of us, adultery is the least objectionable form of sexual misbehavior. We have even dressed it up in a rather attractive word. "What are they doing?" "Oh, they are having an 'affair'." It is almost expected in our society. If you let your eyes wander at the grocery checkout counter, you see magazines that treat the endless escapades of the stars as though they were the normal pattern of life. Extramarital sex is not an "affair"; it is adultery. It is adulterating something beautiful and precious. It is soiling something clean, and God says, "I hate it."

Why not prohibit bestiality in the Ten Commandments? Now there is a nasty sexual sin. But God chooses adultery to underline the fact that sexual activity should take place within the confines of a lifelong binding commitment between a man and a woman. Second, adultery is not merely a misuse of our sexuality, a perversion, but rather it is a breaking of faith. If I have given myself to a woman—whether I stood up before a church and said it or in an intimate conversation in the dark of the night—and then have intercourse with another woman, I have broken my word of faith. Suppose I say, "I am yours completely," and then say, "Hey, I really didn't mean that. I have these sexual needs and this pretty girl just went by and…who can fight that?" But God says, "I hate it."

Do you see what is taking place here? The adulterer says that he or she has a right to supply a perceived sexual need. Throughout the Bible, God says that he is the supplier of our needs. He calls us to surrender our needs into his hands that he might supply them in accordance with his creation standards and his particular plans for our lives. We say, "But God, you don't understand. My spouse and I have been sexually maladjusted for years. Surely I have a right to satisfy this craving. I mean, you gave it to me, God, so surely I have a right to satisfy it." But God responds, "You shall not commit adultery." Clearly, in God's sight, keeping faith with one to whom I have given myself and refusing to crush her in order to meet my supposed needs is more important than any personal right I think I have. When we follow God's plan and life in faithful surrender of our needs to a spouse, we are on the way to understanding what love really is.

So we start out with gratitude to those who have given us life. We move on to an appreciation for the physical life of another. We go on with an appreciation of sexual fidelity that says, "God is the supplier of my needs." Then we move to an appreciation for the property of another. The same theme is continuing: My desire for things does not justify my taking your things. Yahweh is the supplier, not me. What comes from his hand is blessing, while what I grab with my hands is cursed. So your stuff is safe with me. Your property is not mine to use as I wish.

Some very interesting revisions of this command have been proposed in recent years. It has been said that if my loved one is dying and a drug is available which might cure her, but it is too expensive (because of the supposed greed of the drug company), then love justifies my stealing of it. Some have said that if the rich have oppressed me and taken what I think is rightfully mine, then I have a perfect right to steal it back. But God says no. This is not an excuse for injustice, economic or otherwise. God is a God of justice, and he will not put up with oppression forever. But the question is whether my perception of injustice warrants my taking the scales of justice into my own hand. The answer is that it must not. When I decide on the individual level that I have a right to supply my needs with your property, it is all over. It is all over for me, because I no longer trust God to supply my needs and no longer trust him with my life. But beyond that, it is all over for society, because no society can long exist in which its people cannot trust each other.

If your neighbor can trust you with his property, can he trust you with his reputation? "You shall not bear false witness against your neighbor." It took me a long time to really catch this one, because I thought it said, "Thou shalt not lie," but it doesn't. Read it again carefully: "You shall not bear false witness against your neighbor." The focus is not on my integrity, but the way I handle the integrity of others. You see, I can tell the plain truth about you and yet give a very false impression. I can say confidently, "I told the truth," even though my tone of voice, my gestures, and even my word choice implied something quite wrong about you. God says, "What is important is the effect of your words on your neighbor's reputation. Will you seize an opportunity to misrepresent your neighbor to further your own interests?" I believe that is what the commandment means when it prohibits false witness.

All the way through, the focus is on the rights of others and putting those rights before any effort to take care of ourselves. So even though the wording is almost entirely negative ("you shall not"), the intent is very positive. Cherish a parent's right to honor, a neighbor's right to life, a spouse's right to your sexual fidelity, and so on. Never sacrifice any of those rights on the altar of what you conceive to be your own needs.

In the final commandment, Yahweh seems to tie together both sets of commandments, those applying to God and those applying to the neighbor. "You shall not covet anything belonging to your neighbor." Twice in the New Testament, the apostle Paul tells us that covetousness is idolatry (Eph 5:5; Col 3:5). On the surface, that connection does not seem obvious; to have a compulsive desire for something that belongs to someone else does not seem to have anything to do with idol worship. But Paul says this kind of desire is the very thing that drives idol worship. We sell our souls to this world in order to get what we think this world can provide. In short, we have come right back to the first and second commandments. My needs, my desires, my rights—springing up from my greed to get ahead of someone else—have become my gods.

In America, covetousness has become a virtue. We are trained to long for what other people have from childhood. If we are to get free of that, both individually and collectively, God must do a deep work in our hearts. I am impressed that in almost every interview of someone who grew up during the Great Depression, they say, "Well, I guess we were really poor, but we didn't know it." The advertising media make all of us feel poor, as if other people have stuff we would obviously be happier if we had.

I drive through the suburban areas of our large cities and see neighborhoods fueled by covetousness. How big a house must we have, anyway? How many modern amenities must we have? It is amazing how many things I can get along without until you move in next door and show me what you have. Then the "poor me" syndrome takes over, and I sell my soul to match or surpass your lifestyle. It is not surprising that our nation has become the largest debtor nation in the world—our covetousness must be fed at all costs, including the cost of insurmountable public debt. The tenth commandment is talking about that, and all of us need to think seriously and take decisive action to scale back our lifestyles and expectations in order to get ourselves out of the horrible bondage of debt brought on by our covetousness.

I cannot say that there is a certain level of material prosperity beyond which a Christian cannot go, but every one of us who calls ourselves Christian must do whatever it takes to break the bonds of covetousness. One person has suggested that we determine the minimum that we need in order to live—in terms of possessions, house, car, and so forth—and then scale that back by 10 percent. That might be a good first step. In any case, I firmly believe that we must seriously look at our lives and say, "What must I do to get out from under this? What can I do without? What should I do without?"

All of these commands, the basic principles of life as Yahweh designed it, are saying one thing: Let the transcendent, holy God take his rightful place in your life. Shift the focus off of yourself and the supplying of your needs, and put it on him and others. Abandon yourself in trust of God, letting him supply your needs, and discover the freedom that will allow you to find yourself in giving yourself away.

## Questions for Personal Study or Discussion

1. List as many of the Ten Commandments as you can recall from memory and then check your list against the actual Bible text. Did you forget or change the meaning of some of them?

2. Dr. Oswalt has suggested some ways in which we as Christians can "make God's name empty." Suggest some other ways. How can we avoid doing this?

3. The first commandment, which establishes the worship of one God, makes Judaism a form of monotheism (a religion of one god). What other two world religions are forms of monotheism?

4. Some people scorn the idea of having to conform to a list of dos and don'ts, but how do these commandments reinforce what we have learned about God?

5. Americans probably disregard the fourth commandment (about keeping Sabbath) more than any other. Why are some reasons for this? If you recall a time when this was not so, what do you think changed?

6. People who are scrupulous to observe holy standards of conduct can swing too far the other way, into legalism. What daily spiritual disciplines might help you to avoid this?

# CHAPTER 10

# Revelation of Yahweh's Principles
## —Part 3

## The Stipulations of the Covenant (20:3–23:33)

*Interlude 20:18–26*

Bible scholars have raised many questions about the sequence of events in chapters 19 and 20 of Exodus; some believe that these accounts are arranged topically rather than chronologically. But as the text now stands at the beginning of chapter 20, Moses is at the bottom of the mountain and Yahweh is speaking the Ten Commandments aloud in the hearing of all the people. This would be what Moses referred to in Deuteronomy 4:12–13, where he says that of all the people in the world, the Israelites alone have actually heard God speaking. But Exodus 20:18ff suggests that the experience was too much for them. The idea of the transcendent God actually breaking through the barriers of time and space and addressing them was so overwhelming that they could not bear it. Any of us who have ever had a vivid experience of God's presence can relate to this. There was both a sense of overwhelming attraction and terror. Fire is an apt symbol for what they saw: attractive and frightening all at once.

So the people broke into the presentation of the covenant stipulations (20:18–19) and asked Moses to listen to the specific examples and report to them what God had said. Moses agreed to this—that is, he agreed to become their mediator (vv 20–21). This may be a pivotal moment. Up to this point, Moses had been their leader, but now he becomes something more than that. As their mediator, Moses bears the people on his heart before God, and he carries God in his heart and mind for them.

This incident may explain words of warning found in verses 22–26. The first relates to their having heard God's voice. Yahweh says that this experience should be evidence enough that he is not one more of the gods, so they should no longer worship such idols (vv 22–23). The second warning deals with place of sacrifice, i.e., the place of mediation (vv 24–26). Yahweh's point seems to be that, just as they are not to make idols, neither should their altars be modeled on elaborate pagan plans. Intricate rituals and elaborate altars will not bring Yahweh down to them. Either he is already present through the exercise of his mercy, freely extended to repentant, believing worshipers, or he is far away because of their proud, hard, self-serving natures. In either case, any attempt at manipulation would only drive him farther away (see Mic 6:6–8).

*Specific examples 21:1–23:19*
In this section of the stipulations (21:1–23:19), God gives specific examples of ways in which the principles of the covenant might work out in actual life situations. These examples are not meant to cover all of life nor every situation we might encounter, but they are representative. The specific examples advance the overall purpose of the covenant: learning about the character of Yahweh and his intention for life by living out godly behavior. As specific

as the Ten Commandments are as basic principles, recognizable examples are needed. In this section that deficiency—if indeed it is a deficiency—is addressed.

The examples are not grouped in neatly defined categories; in fact, there is a fair amount of mixing of categories. The same editorial pattern appears in other collections of commandments elsewhere in the Bible (e.g., Lev 19). The point is that obedience to God, the pursuit of his character, cannot be neatly codified; it involves a holistic transformation of our lives.

But that phrase "our lives" may raise a question. Does any of this material have real relevance for us in the twenty-first century? Maybe we grant the point made in an earlier chapter—that the stipulations of the covenant were given to demonstrate to the Israelites what God's character is—but surely we have a lot of revelation subsequent to the covenant to amply illustrate that point. And maybe we grant that these stipulations were also given to show the Israelites what sort of lives they needed to live in order to be that "holy nation" promised in Exodus 19:6; but again, we have a lot of admonition and instruction in later parts of the Bible that illustrate what a holy life consists of. So can we not just skip Exodus 21–23 as superfluous ancient history?

While it is true that other later parts of the Bible give us a lot of information about the character of God and the character he expects of us as his people, these chapters (and subsequent repetitions of these commands, such as we find in Leviticus, parts of Numbers, and much of Deuteronomy) are God's inspired Word, which he has caused to be preserved. The church has recognized through the ages that these commands are the fundamental yardstick of Christian life and belief. While we do not say these chapters are uniquely relevant to us today, neither can they be ignored. They have things to teach us that are not taught in precisely this way elsewhere in the Scriptures, and we are the poorer in our faith if we do not pay attention to them.

### Types of Laws

That being said, let me see if I can provide a bit of a guide through their complexities. First of all, we should note that three types of laws are scattered through the various groups. Identifying them will help us in evaluating what applies more directly, and less directly, to us today.

**Ceremonial law** is the first type, and the one that has the least direct application to us. Ceremonial law determines whether a person can participate in worship ceremonies or other community activities. Transgressing these laws, or engaging in these kinds of behaviors, basically means that the transgressor is excluded from the community's ritual life for a period of time. The law often stipulates that the person must engage in some sort of cleansing activity during that time to render them ritually clean again. Essentially, that is all there is to such laws. They seldom have any direct application to us because they were object lessons designed to teach a spiritual truth to the ancient Hebrews through their ritual practices. In most cases, these rituals have now been superseded.

Let me illustrate this. Suppose I want to teach my little boy how to add numbers. I say, "Honey, two plus two equals four." Almost certainly, he will respond to that statement with a glazed look because what I have said is actually a rather high-level abstraction. "Two plus two equals four? Daddy, what is a *two*? And what is a *plus*? And an *equals*? And what do you mean by *four*?" So what will I do? I will hold up two of his toy blocks and ask, "How many?" Because he is a bright little boy, he will answer, "Two!" Great! A real genius. Then I put those two blocks behind my back, pick up two more, and ask the same question. Again, he answers, "Two" (perhaps wondering to himself why I did not get that point the first time). But now comes the test. I pull the first two blocks from behind my back and put them next to the second two. "Now how many blocks, my boy? When we put two together with two, how many do we have?" We can see the wheels turning in his head, and finally he spits it out: "Four!" Yes! He has got it. What have I done? I have used physical objects to teach a profound abstract principle: two added to two equals four.

That is what is going on with the ceremonial laws. God is using object lessons to teach very deep spiritual truths. For instance, how serious is sin? Can we just wink at it and have it go away? No, we cannot. Sin is deadly. Only blood, the blood of an innocent victim, can serve to remove its impact from our lives.

But there are two things about object lessons. First of all, they must be done exactly the same way, every time. You cannot take three blocks and five blocks and end up with a sum of four. You could do three and one, but no variation is possible if the principle is to be taught. So it is with the ceremonial laws; they must be done exactly the same way every time. If they are not, the lesson will not be learned.

The second thing about object lessons is that once the principle is finally engrained, the objects are no longer necessary. Now my boy is eighteen years old and going off to college where he is going to study calculus. So what do I send to college with him? Two billion wooden blocks? No, he doesn't need the blocks anymore. He has figured out what the principles are. So it is with the ceremonial laws: They are not for all time, and were not intended to be.

Imagine now these spiritual infants coming out of Egypt. "Children," God says, "some activities and thoughts and attitudes will leave you as clean as the driven snow in my presence, but other attitudes and activities and behaviors will defile you in my presence." That is pretty high-level stuff. Clean, unclean, defiled, profane, and so forth? The lesson becomes all the more complicated when we remember that these concepts had been tangled up with wrong-headed pagan ideas for the previous four centuries. So what do you do? You tell Zeke that he cannot eat pig because if he does, he cannot join the rest of the community in worship. Now is anything intrinsically wrong with pig?[1] Just as there is nothing inherently significant about the blocks I use to teach my son arithmetic, neither was there anything inherently significant about the foods God prohibited to teach moral cleanness and uncleanness.

So what was God doing? At every meal for over a thousand years, Zeke sat down and looked at the table and said, "Rebekah, is this food clean?"

And Rebekah would answer, "Ezekiel, you know I keep a kosher home."

"All right. Let's eat!"

Presumably, in those years, the moral principle has been driven home: A person who has uncleanness in himself cannot live in the presence of a holy God. So Ezekiel and Rebekah will be ready to hear a riveting young Galilean say, "Friends, it is not what goes into your mouth that makes you unclean. It is what comes out of your mouth that does that" (Matt 15:11). Clearly, not eating pig is not going to make you a morally upright person. But equally clearly, you are now ready to say, "That issue of my unclean heart

---

1. Some people think that pork was prohibited because improperly cooked pork can produce muscle disease. However, I think it is difficult to show that many of the rest of the prohibited foods posed health problems. So while there may be some health factors in these ceremonial food laws, I am confident that was not God's primary purpose in them. If it was, why would he allow Christians to eat pork?

has got to be dealt with, because the unclean cannot exist with God." Perhaps then you are ready to hear that young man say that he is the solution to your moral and spiritual uncleanness.

So the ceremonial laws—the food laws, the clothing laws, and all of these other things—relate to spiritual truths that God is trying to teach. The sacrificial laws taught the Hebrews about the high cost of sin and the fact that sin must be forgiven. Finally, in the light of Christ, something clicked and they got the real message. Finally, they saw what the object lessons were all about, and they heard God say in effect, "Now you can throw away the toy blocks. Jesus, who is the fulfillment of all this truth, has come." So the ceremonial laws had to be kept, and they had to be kept very precisely, but they were not for all time.

The important thing for us to think about as we encounter these kinds of laws is what they were meant to teach. Is my life demonstrating the truth of this teaching? Am I engaging in activities or thoughts that are manifestly unclean? Do I treat the sacrifice of Christ as something essentially trivial and meaningless? Am I crucifying him afresh by my careless behavior? Am I making every effort to exclude sin (as represented by infectious skin diseases, mold, yeast, and so on) from my life?

**Civil law.** The second kind of law found in these specific examples may be labeled civil law. Here a principle with eternal relevance is expressed in the context of behaviors that were common in ancient times, not in all times. So with civil laws we must separate the temporary container from the eternal truth it contained. The container was time-bound, but what is contained has just as much significance for you and me as it did for Ezekiel and Rebekah.

Let me give you an example in the law of the goring ox (Ex 21:29–36). Suppose a person owns an ox, which has always been placid and docile; the owner has never had any trouble with him. But one day a neighbor is walking along a path next to the plot where the ox is grazing. Suddenly, with no warning, the ox lets out a bellow, attacks the neighbor, and kills him. What should be done to the owner of the ox? The law says nothing should be done to him because the owner had no way of knowing such a thing was likely to happen.

On the other hand, suppose this ox had always had a mean streak. The owner knew enough never to turn his back on him and not to go too near him without a good-sized club. Suppose that ox is grazing and the neighbor walks down the path and the ox kills him. What now? Now the law says that owner has murdered his neighbor because he knew that ox was a potential killer and did not tie him up securely.

We might say, "Well, that is an interesting bit of trivia, that example of ancient jurisprudence, but it has no application to my life." Think about it and you'll realize a timeless principle resides inside that quaint container of a law about oxen. The principle is that knowledge equals responsibility.

I don't have oxen, but I do have a car. Suppose as I pull out of the driveway in my car some morning, I put the brakes on and feel the pedal go almost to the floor before the car stops Then I look back on my driveway and see a pool of dark fluid there. I am late as usual, in a terrible hurry, so I go on up the street. As I come over the top of a hill, I see you starting through the intersection at the bottom, so I put on my brakes. The pedal goes right the floor, and I do not slow down at all but actually pick up speed. I hit you and kill you. Whatever the courts might say, God says that knowledge is responsibility. I knew my brakes were faulty and I didn't do anything about it, so I murdered you.

So the objective for us in these ancient civil laws is to extract the eternal principle from its time-bound container. The penalty for violating ceremonial law was simply separation from the worshiping community. With civil laws, the punishment was generally in kind. That is, if you misappropriated property, then you had to restore property, perhaps with some sort of interest. If you injured someone, you had to pay an amount of money equal to the injury. If you killed someone, your own life was forfeited. Punishment was in kind. Interestingly, in other law codes of the Ancient Near East, the punishments for property crimes tended to be more severe. For instance, in many cases theft was punishable by death. By contrast, in his covenant with Israel, Yahweh seems to be saying, "A person has a right to have their property protected, but no property is more valuable than people."

**Moral law.** The third class of laws may be labeled moral law. Whereas civil and ceremonial laws tend to be stated as cases ("If so and so is done, then so and so shall be done to the perpetrator"), moral law is normally stated in simple absolute commands: "You shall... You shall not..." These tend to be offenses against God or against life itself. If a punishment is specified, it is normally death. These eternal principles are stated in plain Hebrew, meant to stand for all time, in all places. So, for example, "You shall not permit a sorceress to live. Whoever lies with an animal shall be put to death. Whoever sacrifices to any god, except Yahweh alone, forfeits his or her life to God." (Ex. 22:18–20). It does not matter what your situation is—whether rich, poor, or in between—do not do it. It does not matter what your location is—Egypt, America, or the North Pole—don't practice sorcery, or bestiality, or false worship.

But this raises the question of the death penalty. If a moral principle is being stated for all time, should we not thereby enforce the same penalty? It seems to me that two extremes need to be avoided. Both of them relate to linking the prohibition and the punishment inseparably.

On the one hand, it is not necessary to enforce the punishment because we insist that the Old Testament moral law is still valid. On the other hand, we should not say that since we are unwilling to carry out capital punishment today, the moral principles do not apply either. The first position was that of the church elders in Salem, Massachusetts, when they killed several women who had been convicted of being witches. Few modern Christians believe they are "the chosen people of God," as the Salem elders mistakenly believed. The Israelites were unique in their relationship to God and in their significance for the world. They had to survive as the carriers of God's revelation to the world, so radical penalties were necessary to preserve them and the revelation they had received. Although we are the successors of Israel and share in their blessings, we are not chosen people in that unique historical sense. The revelation has been completed in Jesus Christ; therefore, such radical penalties (especially given human sinfulness and the ease with which we can be misled) are no longer necessary. This is the point that Jesus seems to have been making in the incident recorded in John 8, where he told the Jewish leaders that whoever was without sin should stone the adulterous woman.

On the other hand, even though we would not now apply the death penalty for these sins, let us not jump to the conclusion that such behaviors are no longer sins. This is the position of some modern people who say that "barbarous" death penalties show that these laws were just the creations of some ancient, fearful, unenlightened tribes-people. But that is not the case. The death penalty was necessary because of the precarious situation of the

Hebrew people and the need to protect not only them but the revelation itself. Unless the Hebrew people were protected from the alluring paganism all around them, the unique revelation of God would have been lost. Moreover, the fact that these sins were punishable by death underlined their fundamental seriousness and eternal implications. We are not talking about a transient object lesson but an eternal principle. So the death penalty in that situation underlined for them (and by extension for all of us) the fact that murder is serious business forever and ever.

As we noted at the outset, laws of all three types—ceremonial, civil, and moral—are tangled up together in this section of Exodus. The laws of each type are not all grouped together, but scattered throughout. Surely this is because one cannot separate the activities of life when one belongs to God. When you belong to God, everything you do is significant to that relationship. What I do on Monday is just as significant as what I do on Sunday. By the same token, what I do on Sunday is just as significant as what I do on Monday. It all goes together. In the ancient world, it was much easier to compartmentalize your life: what you did with the gods was over here, and what you did with people was over there. The gods might have some interest in how you treated people, but it was a distant, passive kind of interest. Yahweh says, "No way. I am the Lord of all of life. Every aspect of your life belongs to me, and all your behavior is an expression of who you are in me."

With this introduction to the types of law we will encounter, let us turn now to the actual examples themselves.

**The rights of servants (21:1–11).** It is surely significant that the very first specific examples deal with the rights of servants. We who are used to thinking in terms of social hierarchies might expect that we would begin with the rights of masters or owners. But Yahweh does not value persons as the world does. The gods of this world clearly value the rich, the powerful, the beautiful, the contributors, but not Yahweh. He values all people because they are created in his own image. So he has a special concern for those least able to care for themselves and defend their rights as persons.

**The rights of those who have experienced violence (21:12–27).** If someone commits an act of violence toward anyone else, whether slave or free, what are the rights of the person who has been injured? Here we see that while violence is not allowed to go unpunished, God imposes limits on how far the vengeance can go. Just because a person has acted violently toward another does not mean that the perpetrator loses all rights. One thinks here of mobs tearing apart someone who has hurt another. Yahweh is concerned for all persons.

**The rights of those who have suffered a loss (21:28–22:15).** Here is where the law of the goring ox occurs (21:28–32). Like that one, a major concern of the laws in this section is the establishment of responsibility and a careful correlation of the degree of responsibility with the measure of retribution. In cases where the responsibility is contested, the contestants were to come before God, where a decision would be rendered, probably by the casting of the sacred lots, Urim and Thummim (e.g., Num 27:21). Interestingly, even if you did not know that a loss had occurred because of you, you often bear some level of responsibility. You are not normally let off scot-free. So if you borrow a work animal and it is injured or dies, it does not matter whether you actually caused the loss or not; you have to replace it (22:14). But again, there are limits on retribution. For instance, if a homeowner kills a thief in the night as the theft is occurring, he is not held responsible for the death. However, if he recognizes the thief the next day and kills him then, he is considered a murderer (22:2–3).

While there is a concern for scrupulous fairness, there is yet a deeper concern underlying all of this: a profound conviction of personal worth, whether that of the one wronged or the one who has committed the wrong. Ultimately, persons are more important than property.

**Miscellaneous commands for conduct (22:16–23:9).** While some commentators say that the common theme among these laws is social justice, they seem to me to cover a wider area than that and thus provide evidence that covenant faithfulness to God cannot be divided up into neat categories. For instance, there are the prohibitions of sorcery, bestiality, and idolatry (22:18–20), as well as other commands of a moral nature. To be sure, social justice is prominent. So God's people are not to take advantage of the immigrant (22:21–24; 23:9) or those who are forced to borrow money (22:25–27). Similarly, judicial corruption that results in a miscarriage of justice, especially for the poor, is sternly forbidden (23:1–3, 6–8). But perhaps the element that binds all these together is the statement found in 22:31: "You shall be holy men for me." To be sure, the rest of the verse talks about not eating the meat of an animal that wild animals have torn, i.e., an animal that died with its blood still in it. This appears to restrict holiness to the ceremonial. However, I think a case can be made that this principle is what ties the apparently disparate commandments together: A person who belongs exclusively to God will not seduce a virgin, condone sorcery, commit bestiality, practice idolatry, oppress an immigrant or a borrower, withhold the stated offerings from God, and so forth. In other words, holiness is expressed in daily behavior.

**Commandments for worship (23:10–19).** Here is another somewhat miscellaneous collection, although all connected to ceremonies. The first and second commands (23:10–12) relate to the Sabbath year and the Sabbath day. In each instance, the Sabbath principle is the same: Every seventh day and every seventh year, you let the land rest. This reminded the faithful Hebrew that he was not the ultimate supplier of his own needs, but the Lord, Yahweh, was. We can imagine an Israelite landowner saying, "I can't afford to do that. I'll starve in that seventh year!" But God says to him and us, "Do you love me? Do you trust me? Am I the supplier of your needs?"

A second major topic is the three annual Jewish feasts. These occurred about April 1 when the barley harvest was complete and the wheat harvest was starting; about June 1, when the wheat harvest was complete; and about September 20, when the grape harvest was complete. It is no accident that these festivals occurred at the same time the Jews' pagan neighbors were engaging in fertility rites, intended to secure and maintain the fecundity of Mother Earth. God's law diverted his people from those compelling and exciting events. As later instructions would make clear, the last thing the Hebrews were to do in their own festivals was to try to manipulate the fertility of the earth, to somehow make God bless them through magical rites. Instead, these were to be festivals of remembrance and thanksgiving. The Israelites were to remember how Yahweh had blessed them in the past, as at the Passover and in the wilderness. They were to give thanks for blessings past and present, trusting that those same blessings would extend from his gracious, transcendent hand in the future.

**Stipulations Yahweh places on himself (23:20–33).** Now that we have heard the stipulations that Yahweh placed on his people as their part of the covenant, we hear what he promises to do, i.e., the covenant obligations he places on himself. He had shown them that to be in covenant with him would mean that they would act like he does. "I care about persons. I am honest. I am pure. I am clean. I don't manipulate people. This is what kind of a person I am. Your part of the covenant is to live like that." If they agreed, Yahweh promised to do eight things for them.

First, he would take them to the land he had prepared for them (v 20). That is, they would not languish and die in that howling wilderness.

Second, no adversaries or enemies would be able to defeat them on the way (v 22). Even though they were a ragtag group of refugees with little military training or organization, God would continue to defend them, just as he had protected them from the Amalekites (17:8–13).

Third, God would wipe out the inhabitants of the land of Canaan so the Israelites could settle there (vv 23, 27–31). Fourth, he would provide their basic needs (bread and water, v 25). Fifth, he would give them health (v 25). Sixth, he would give fertility to the women (v 26). Seventh, he would give the people long life (v 26). Eighth, he would extend their borders to their natural geographic limits (v 31). In short, Yahweh would provide for every need they might have.

But scattered throughout all these promises are repeated admonitions—admonitions reflecting the first (and to some extent the second) commandment. The promises are contingent on continued obedience to the commands of the covenant, particularly the commandment concerning exclusive loyalty to Yahweh. The Israelites must not worship the gods of the Canaanites. In fact, they must actively root out that religion and its practices. The reason for this is clear: If the Canaanites and their religion remain, they will lead the people into sin (vv 21, 24, 32–33).

Why was there still a danger of this? As we noted earlier, the religion of this world is very attractive to us humans because it gives us the illusion of control. But that is precisely the root of all sin—the belief that my desires and my will are supreme, and I have an absolute right to fulfill those desires in any way that I can. Idolatrous religion is a sin, not simply because it is wrong, but also because it says things about God and reality that are not so, and it justifies the rest of the catalog of sins, all based in self-serving.

## The Sealing of the Covenant (24:1–18)

We come now to the final act of the covenant, the formal ceremony of acceptance and sealing. The steps that Moses and the people go through here would have been found in most covenant ceremonies at the time.

First, Moses secured the verbal agreement of the people. He reminded them what the covenant terms were and asked whether they were willing to do those things. They responded that of course they would. Yahweh was not asking anything unreasonable, and they certainly wanted to enjoy his promises.

Then Moses built an altar and twelve pillars according to the twelve tribes (v 4). What were the pillars about? Remember that in the standard covenant form, all the relevant gods were called upon to witness the acceptance of the covenant. That could hardly be a part of this covenant, in which no other god but Yahweh could be recognized. So instead of having some pagan deities witness this covenant, Moses set up historical markers to represent the twelve Hebrew tribes. God had met his people in time and space, something unique had happened here, and these pillars were historical records of that event. They were visible witnesses to the fact that something important took place right here.

I can imagine years later: Uncle Isaac packs up all the kids on the camels and says, "We are going on a trip."

When they got there, I am sure the kids were distinctly un-impressed. But then they saw the twelve stones and asked, "What are those for?"

"This is where your fathers said, 'We are going to serve God, so help us God. This is the place where God stepped into our time and space, into our lives, and forever changed them. This is the place where God made us his.'"

Those twelve pillars testified that at a certain place and in a certain time, God entered our daily existence and changed everything. They were the earnest of what God would do in Jesus Christ. In Jesus, God would enter time and space in the form of a particular man, who lived in a particular part of the world at a particular time. He was the final revelation of God for the world.

Next, Moses sacrificed twelve bulls and threw half of the blood on the altar. What was that about? To understand it, we must read on. Moses took the Book of the Covenant in which he had written what we have in chapters 20–23, and read it to the people. Why? Because a covenant had to be a written document. This is a deadly serious moment, and there must be no possibility of misunderstanding.

The people had not changed their minds. Why would they? God was not asking anything bizarre, like jumping straight up twenty feet and staying there for five minutes. He was not asking anything cruel, like eating your children. He was not asking anything destructive, like eating dirt three times a day. What he was asking was straightforward and sensible. So of course they said yes a second time.

Notice what Moses then did. He threw the other half of the blood, the half that was not thrown on the altar, on the people. As he did so, he said, "Behold, the blood of the covenant." I suspect that as that blood dripped down their faces, the hair on the back of their necks began to stand up and they said, "Wait a minute, what did we just agree to?" You see, this was a blood oath. In a covenant ceremony between two individuals, they took a sacrificial animal and split it in two. Then they laid the two bloody halves of the animal down on the ground, the two parties to the covenant linked arms, and they stepped in between those bloody halves. Standing there, they said to each other, "May God do so to me if I ever break this covenant."

That is what was said by throwing half of the blood on the altar: "May God strike God dead, if God ever breaks this covenant." It is the same thing that he had done years earlier with Abraham (Gen 15). Referring to that incident, the writer of Hebrews said, "God swore by himself there being none higher" (Heb 6:13). In the same way, when half the blood was thrown on the people, they were saying, "May God strike us dead if we ever break this covenant." If the hair wasn't standing up on the backs of their necks, it should have been, for they had a problem—a big problem—and they did not know it.

Within five weeks, this solemn covenant was broken and they were dancing around an idol, praising it for having delivered them from Egypt. They could not keep the covenant for five weeks, let alone forever. But they did not know that at this point. They were like a newly converted Christian who thinks all he has to do is make up his mind. Little did they know that they were entering a saga of unimaginable failure and unimaginable grace, which is what the rest of the Old Testament is about.

You see, once they had broken the covenant, God was legally required to enforce that blood curse upon them. Technically, from the time of the golden calf onward, Yahweh is violating the covenant by not destroying the Israelites. Yet for fourteen hundred years, while Israel was continually breaking their covenant, God kept fulfilling his covenant promises to them whenever there was the least pretext for doing so. This is why you have the repeated phrase in the Psalms and elsewhere in the Old Testament, "O give thanks to the Lord, for he is good and his mercy [*hesed*] endures forever" (e.g., Ps 106:1).

But how could he keep on doing that? God cannot violate his own laws of cause and effect. But it is even more serious than that, because not only should the Israelites who broke the covenant be destroyed, but all of us should be. "The person who sins will die," the covenant said, and that is to die eternally. So what could God do? He could not say, "We'll just suspend the law of cause-and-effect in this instance." If he did, the whole universe would fly to pieces.

So come with me to the upper room. The disciples know something strange is going on here. They do not understand what this "cross" is that Jesus has been going on about for the last six months. They cannot believe that the Messiah, of all people, should have to die. Yet they realize that some sort of a climax is about to be reached. It has been a strange, strange evening. Jesus has said they are going to betray him, but why would they do that, for heaven's sake? Jesus is going to be the emperor of the universe, so who would betray him?

In the course of the Passover meal, Jesus passes the cup of wine called the Qiddush (the Sacred Cup), and as that cup is going around, Jesus says, "Behold the blood of the covenant. Behold my blood of the Covenant." Do you think those Jews have any trouble making the connection? No, in a flash their minds go back to Exodus 24, and the pronouncement of the blood oath: "Behold the blood of the covenant." In other words, Jesus was saying, "I am the sacrifice that satisfies the old covenant." The old covenant had been crying out for the just punishment of these covenant-breakers for fourteen hundred years. But there in the upper room, God responded, "No, I don't have to kill them. Not if I die in their place, and satisfy the old covenant."

Moreover, when Jesus died on the cross, he became the sacrificial animal to ratify a new covenant. He is the animal split in half; it is his body that lies on the ground so that you and I and God could link arms, step through, and God could write his covenant on our hearts (Jer 31:31). "Behold my blood of the covenant." That's what was happening when Jesus passed the cup. He was saying, "I am the fulfillment of all that the old covenant called for and you couldn't obey. I am the beginning of the new covenant, which is written on your heart, in the power and the life of the Holy Spirit, that you might do what your heart longs to do."

Remember that the one difference between the old covenant and the new, as Jeremiah makes clear, is where it is written. With the exception of the ceremonial laws, the content of the new covenant is the same as the content of the old covenant. Yahweh did not change the content because he did not change his character. He did not change the quality of life that he expected from the believer. The content is the same in the old covenant as it is in the new. The life expected of the believer in the Old Testament is the same life expected of the believer in the New Testament. What changed? The old covenant that they broke was external to them, outside of them. The new covenant is written on our hearts. The Holy Spirit has put the covenant inside of us. We have an ability to follow God's instructions that the ancient Jew never had, because Christ has given us his Holy Spirit. That is the difference.

Well, what is next? A meal. Seventy elders, representing the people, were invited up onto the mountain to eat a meal with God (vv 9–11). What does that signify? That the goal of the covenant is fellowship. Why did God deliver the people from Egypt? To bring them to himself (19:4). Why did Jesus die on the cross and rise again from the dead? So that we could be restored to fellowship with God, so that his presence would bless us instead of destroying us. The whole point of salvation is fellowship. God did it all so that we could come home to him (1 John 1:3). God did it all so that we could live in his arms. God did it all so that we could know him as Father. This fellowship meal, as the final step of sealing the covenant, underlines that fact.

Interestingly, the text says, "And they saw God" (24:10). Whatever else that means, it emphasizes the fellowship element. God was not just an idea, he was really there among them. Now those of us with a little familiarity with the book of Exodus are probably remembering chapter 33 where Yahweh said to Moses, "Nobody can see my face and live." So whatever these elders saw, they did not see the face of God; but they did see something, a visible experience of God's presence. Notice that there is no description of God! The closest the text comes to such a description is a remark about the heavenly appearance of the pavement under his feet! It is as though words break down at the pavement. When people later asked the elders to describe what they saw, they could only get as far as the pavement.

It was the same thing with Isaiah, many centuries later. Isaiah came drifting out of the temple with heaven all over his face, saying, "I saw the Lord." But what description do we have of what Isaiah saw? "The hem of his robe filled the temple." The capacity of words to describe that vision broke down at the hem of the robe. This is the One who wants fellowship with us, One for whom there really are no words. He is not some useful little idol. He is the Holy One, and it is his glory, not that of any other, that fills the earth.

# Questions for Personal Study or Discussion

1. How is the short form of God's stipulations (the Ten Commandments) different from the long form in Exodus 21:1–23:19? What are some advantages and disadvantages of having these two renditions of the law?

2. Case law uses a real-life examples to show how a legal principle should be applied in our daily activities. Skim-read the case laws of Exodus 20:18–23:19 and list some of its examples of the Ten Commandments in action.

3. For each example you listed under #1 above, list a comparable situation from modern life where the same principle should be applied.

4. Compare your answers under #1 and #2. What do these cases reveal about the character and moral priorities of God? Note that while daily activities change from one era of history to another, God's principles remain the same.

5. Dr. Oswalt says that Old Testament ceremonial laws were like toy blocks that our heavenly Father used to teach basic truths to the Israelites. For this reason, ceremonial laws "are not for all time, and were not intended to be." What are some Hebrew ceremonial laws that various Christian groups have tried to revive?

6. Review Dr. Oswalt's explanation of a Hebrew civil law concerning goring by an ox. Imagine some other current situations in which the underlying principle (personal

accountability for injury or damage caused by our property) might be applied. Explain why this principle is still valid—or not.

7. The death penalty was often exacted of people who violated moral law in Old Testament times (e.g., worshiping an idol, engaging in perverse sex acts). Dr. Oswalt says this "was necessary because of the precarious situation of the Hebrew people and the need to protect not only them but the revelation itself." In some countries today, Islamic moral law (*shariah*) still carries a death penalty. Do you think it is justified for the same reason?

CHAPTER 11

# The Revelation of His Presence
## (25:1–40:38)—Part 1

We might expect the book of Exodus to end after the covenant meal in chapter 24. After all, the people have been delivered from bondage, and in the process they have learned of Yahweh's power and providence. Now they have entered into a covenant with him and in so doing have begun to learn his principles and to be delivered from their spiritual darkness. So let's get on to the real goal and march into the Promised Land, right?

Well, no, the book does not end here. Why not? Because the real goal of the deliverance has not yet been achieved—fellowship between the Creator and his creatures. As real as the problems of bondage and spiritual darkness are, the most serious human problem is alienation from God. So God delivers us in order to bring us home to himself. He delivers us so that he can come down off the mountain to take up residence in our camp.[1] But even that is not enough for him; his final goal is residence in our hearts (Eph 2:22).

How important is this theme to Yahweh? Important enough that the description of the tabernacle is given twice: 24:12–31:18

---

1. The Hebrew word translated "tabernacle" is *mishkan*, which is a noun made from a verb meaning "to dwell." So a *mishkan* is a "dwelling place."

and 35:1–40:38. He seems like a first-time homeowner: he cannot get enough of going over the blueprints. In fact, the second iteration is a report of how the complex was built, which means that it is out of chronological sequence. The tabernacle was only completed on the first day of the first month of the second year after leaving Egypt (40:1), but parts of Leviticus occurred before that date (Lev 26:46). Why this alteration of the sequence? Surely it is to highlight the importance of the erection of the tabernacle as the true goal of the deliverance from Egypt.

If today you know that you are redeemed from sin, even if you know that you are committed and empowered by the Holy Spirit to live like Christ, but you are not experiencing the reality of his presence, you have not received your full inheritance. The Bible is about the *presence* of God, not his *presents*. The Christian life is not about having my name written on a privileged list somewhere. It is not even about living as righteously as I know how to live. It is about having God live within me. God lives in a heart that has been cleansed through regeneration from the sins of the past. God lives in a heart that is cleansed because of the Holy Spirit's power. Those steps of spiritual preparation are not the important thing, but rather the fact that God does live there. That is why Jesus says, "If you just sweep the house out, and kick the devils out, but don't let the Holy Spirit come in to fill the place with His presence, you are going to have a worse problem in short order, because the devils are going to come back through the plumbing. And they are going to say, 'Isn't this a great clean house to live in?'" (Matt 12:43–45). The demon of self-righteousness, religious pride, and all of those horrible, clean, and yet godless things, comes to live in us.

## Chapters 25–40: A Survey

Before we look at this material in some detail, I want to give you a bit of a roadmap of what occurs in these chapters. After the fellowship meal, which occurred part way up the mountain, Yahweh told Moses to go the rest of the way to the top. He did not tell him why, so of course Moses could not tell the elders why either. But he put Aaron and Hur in charge while he was gone. This all occurs at the end of chapter 24.

Immediately in chapter 25 we learn that God called Moses to the top of the mountain to give him instructions for the building of a sanctuary and instituting a priesthood to serve in the sanctuary. In general, the instructions Yahweh gave move outward, beginning with the covenant box[2] that stood in the innermost part of the tent and concluding with the appointment of those who would erect the complex. One possible reason for beginning with the covenant box is that it was the place where the covenant's stone tablets are to be kept. The details of the instructions go like this:

Chapter 25: the dimensions and details of the covenant box, the table for the bread of the presence, and the lampstand. That is, this chapter describes the furniture of the tabernacle.

Chapter 26: the dimensions and details of the posts and draperies that formed the sanctuary tent itself.

Chapter 27: specifications for the bronze altar that stood in the courtyard in front of the tent, and the posts and curtains that formed the courtyard.

---

2. *Ark* was simply a word for "box" (the meaning of the Hebrew word) in 1611 English. "Ark of the covenant" has come to have worshipful connotations (while confusing whole generations of children who have wondered why there was a boat—remember Noah's Ark—in the tabernacle) but it was simply a gold-covered box.

Chapter 28: details about the materials and design of the garments of the priests who would serve in this sanctuary.

Chapter 29: instructions for sanctifying the priests.

Chapter 30: additional items (perhaps reported here because they were uniquely associated with the priesthood): the incense altar, the bronze laver, preparation of the sacred oil and incense.

Chapter 31: the appointment of Spirit-filled craftsmen Bezalel and Oholiab to carry out the work of construction.

Interestingly, all these instructions conclude with a reiteration of the importance of keeping the Sabbath.

So here we have seven whole chapters devoted to instructions for building a sanctuary and sanctifying the priests who would serve in it. Up through chapter 24, the Hebrew words for *holy* and *holiness* have only appeared seven times in the book. In chapters 25–31, these words appear more than thirty-five times. Like the dirt around the burning bush in chapter 3, everything associated with this remarkable Being who intended to come down off the mountain and live in the middle of the camp was touched by his uniqueness.

Certainly, we need hardly anything more to close the book, right? It seems logical just to get a brief report of how the Hebrews carried out Yahweh's instructions and his consequent taking up residence within the tabernacle. But no, something else is reported, something that was actually taking place at the very time Moses was receiving God's instructions. Chapters 32–34 report this horrifying event.

At the very time that Yahweh was giving Moses instructions for what needed to take place so that he could live in their midst, the Israelites were taking matters into their own hands. They decided that they needed God's presence in their midst, and Moses was so long delayed that they assumed he was not coming back.

So they instructed Aaron to make them an idol, which Aaron seems to have had no qualms about doing. They broke the covenant that they had sworn in blood to keep. Instead of bringing God nearer, this actually drove him farther away. Chapters 33 and 34 describe this and culminate with God's having to unilaterally renew his side of the covenant in chapter 34.

I suspect that it is precisely because of this event that chapters 35–40 repeat the words of chapters 25–31 almost verbatim. The chief difference is this: Whereas the wording in Exodus 25–31 said, "You shall…," chapters 35–40 say, "They did…." In other words, this is a report that the Israelites obeyed every word of Yahweh's commands the second time around. This is especially obvious in chapters 39 and 40, where the words "as Yahweh commanded Moses" occur over and over. Clearly, after the people tried to supply their needs in their own way and got themselves into deep trouble, the narrator of Exodus says they started over again and did it just the way they were supposed to have done it in the first place, with wonderful results.

Of course, there may be another reason why this repetition occurs. As we noted earlier, when God wants to make a point, he repeats himself. So by repeating this description of the tabernacle, he is saying, "This is important to me. The reality of my presence in your midst is worth talking about twice because this is what it is all about." So these two descriptions of the tabernacle may imply that if we have gotten all the wisdom, had all the experiences, and done everything we were told to do, but do not have the personal reality of the presence of God filling our lives, we have missed the whole point of our journey. That truth is underlined in the climax of the book in chapter 40, where we are told, "The glory of the Lord filled the tabernacle in the midst of the camp."

To put this into the New Testament context, the goal of the cross and the resurrection is Pentecost. We are delivered from the bondage of our sins in order that God the Holy Spirit can take up residence in the tabernacle of our hearts and reproduce the character of God in us.

## The Needs God Was Preparing to Meet

When we look at the instructions that Yahweh gave in chapters 25–31, which were eventually carried out in chapters 35–40, we see that God anticipated the needs that human beings normally have, and he prepared to meet them.

First of all, because we humans are both spirit and body, we need tangibility for our worship. We need something that we can visualize, something we can touch, something that will physically represent God in our midst. We see this throughout human history. People need to build worship centers; we need things that help us visualize what we consider to be the spiritual realities of our world. Why can we not just sit in the middle of a bare desert and think holy thoughts? Because we are not merely spiritual beings. We are both spirit and body. So we need something to see and touch and experience with all of our senses if we are going to worship spiritual reality.

For this reason, there is nothing wrong with building sanctuaries. Some people say, "Well, we shouldn't do that. We ought to have house churches where we just sit in each other's living rooms and worship the invisible God." I do not think that is possible for very long. As human beings, we need to build sanctuaries— tangible holy places. The instinct to build idols comes from this natural human need: We want to make the invisible God visible. God knew this and, although he did not permit his people to make idols of him, he gave them wonderful ways of visualizing his truth in the variety of shapes and forms in the tabernacle.

Second, human beings need to have beauty in their lives. I find this so fascinating. Something in the human heart yearns for beauty and seeks it out. A misshapen jug that tips sideways and has a blob of clay here and a piece of straw sticking out there will still hold water. It does what it is supposed to do, but we are not content with that, are we? Something within us says, "Let's make it symmetrical. Let's put this pleasing curve here, let's roll the lip out in this way, and let's be sure the jug sits up straight." Someone may say, "Well, that's just practicality. A jug will hold more water and hold it more safely if it is symmetrical and vertical." I suppose there is some truth to that, but we all know there is more to our quest for beauty than mere utility. We humans are attracted to things that are aesthetically pleasing, and so God instructed Moses to make things of great beauty to help his people worship him. The variety of colors and design, of decoration and fabric planned for the tabernacle were all meant to answer this need for beauty.

Third, we need activity. We need to be bodily involved when we worship God. We need to do something physical as well as spiritual. We need to be able to say, "I did something to show how precious my God is to me. I used my hands and my feet and my mind. I did something." So God's instructions to Moses had provisions to involve almost everyone in the activities of worship, under the Spirit-filled guidance of Bezalel.

Fourth, we need guidance and protection. This is an uncertain world. We do not know the future, yet we have to make decisions about which way to go. Sometimes the uncertainty is almost paralyzing. I once knew a young seminarian who was very much in love with a beautiful young woman, and she clearly reciprocated his feelings. But he was in a literal agony of indecision because he was not sure she was "the right one." He said to me, "Suppose I marry her and in a year or two someone else comes along that I like better. What then?" So we talked about the true nature of love's self-denial, self-giving, and submission to God's will, as well as the meaning of marital commitment. They eventually married and, so far as I know, have a very successful marriage. But the pain of his uncertainty was real.

The Israelites were in a similar position. They had no road maps through the wilderness. None of them knew how to get from Sinai to Canaan; not one of them had taken this route before. They needed someone or something to show them the way. God knew that and intended that the cloud over the tabernacle would do that very thing. He would lead them if they would only follow his instructions. Not only would the cloud show the way forward, it would also come behind them to protect them from their enemies. We need protection as well as guidance. While this world supports human life, it can also snatch it away in a second. We do not know what natural disasters may come our way or what direction our enemy is coming from. So we each need to know that someone is looking out for us. Without that certainty, we can be consumed with anxiety. God's cloud had provided such protection on that fearful night when the Israelites had the sea before them and the Egyptian army behind them. Exodus 14:19–20 says the cloud stood between them and the Egyptians so they could safely cross. So it would be again if only the Israelites would allow God to provide protection in his way. This idea—that Yahweh is our guide and our protector—must have been on Isaiah's mind hundreds of years later, when he said that Yahweh is our vanguard and our rearguard (Isa 52:12). God goes before us to lead and follows us to protect.

Yahweh knows our needs better than we do, and he can meet them in ways we never could. That is why he called Moses up to the mountain. He said, "Moses, I want to tell you my plans. I want to tell you how I will fulfill the needs of my people." How often you and I hear the Enemy say, "God doesn't care about your needs. God's got his own plans, big plans for saving the world, so he doesn't care about you. Oh, he may lure you on by giving you just enough to get what he wants from you, but he doesn't really care about you. He would let you starve to death if he thought it would make you more religious. He would let you be stripped naked and left homeless if it might make you more spiritual." That is the way the Enemy talks.

You recognize, of course, that that is not a new line. It is the same thing that Satan said to our first mother and father. "He doesn't care about you. He doesn't want you to be wise. He doesn't want you to have beauty or the pleasant sensation of good flavor. He doesn't want you to have any understanding of why some things are right and others are wrong, because if you did, you would be like him. He is not going to let anybody be like him. Oh, no. So when he said you would die if you disobeyed him, that was just a lie to protect himself." Satan has not changed his pitch, because we still fall for it. We conclude that God does not care about our needs, so we try to supply them for ourselves.

No! A thousand times no. God is sensitive to his children's needs, just as a good human father is sensitive to the needs of his children. God knows what we really need and longs to meet those needs if we will let him. So here he knew that the Israelites needed some tangible evidence of his presence in their midst, some beauty in that expression, some personal involvement in worship, and confidence in his guidance and protection. So he called Moses up onto the mountain to describe how he would meet those needs.

"If that were the case," you might respond, "why didn't God tell the people what he was doing? Why didn't he say, 'Now Moses, before you come up here, let's tell them exactly what you are doing and why. Let's explain how long this conference will take, when you will be back, and...'" Why not? Why didn't God tell them?

Surely, one reason is the human heart's desire for control. Something in the human heart says, "O God, tell me your plans, your program, and your schedule so I can sign off on it. I will decide whether I like it and whether I will comply with it. But you have to tell me in advance what you plan to do."

Our relationship with God does not work that way, does it? That is not the way of faith, and salvation is by faith. Faith says, "God, I don't know how you are going to meet my needs, or when you are going to meet my needs, or where you are going to meet my needs, but I believe you will meet them. So the most foolish thing I could do is run ahead of you and try to meet them myself." One of the most important words in the Old Testament is the word *wait*. Why? Because when we wait without knowing when the waiting will end, we surrender our right to control. Oh, how we humans beings hate to give up control! So God keeps maneuvering us into these situations where we are absolutely in no control of anything. We have to wait.

That is what Yahweh did here. He wanted to put the Israelites through the school of faith, so they would be able to say, "Better God's way in his time than my way in my time." Unfortunately, they failed to learn that lesson. We can put ourselves in their sandals, can't we? Moses had been on the burning mountain for nearly six weeks. There was no water there, so any reasonable person knew he had to be dead. What were they going to do? They needed a supernatural power to lead them out of this howling wilderness. They needed a god! They had waited a long time already.

But the last moment we can possibly wait is the next moment before God will act. When you truly come to the point of saying, "I cannot wait one minute longer"—but you do—God shows up with better provision for your needs than you could have imagined. This is why God did not tell Moses or the Israelites what he was going to do on the mountain.

## Meeting Our Needs Our Way

With tragic irony, at the very moment God was giving Moses instructions for the very things they most needed, the Israelites decided they could not wait one moment longer. They moved ahead to meet those needs for themselves. How typical that is of us, and how predictable the results are. The tragedy is that when we try to meet our legitimate needs in our own ways, without depending on God, the result is cursed. God does not have to say in a fit of rage, "I am going to curse those people." Simply because we begin to live in ways God did not plan for us, the result is ruin.

Look at it this way: God made the human body so that it does not respond well to falling off of tall buildings, so he told the Hebrews that they must make a ledge at the edges of the flat roofs of their houses. Suppose someone said, "I don't need to spend my money on roof ledges. I have more fun things to do." So their child falls off. Curse! Not because God arbitrarily said, "I'll make you miserable because you did not obey me," but simply because human beings choose to ignore the realities of how God made our bodies and the force of gravity.

I think another factor was at work in the particular setting of God's giving of his law to the Hebrews. The covenant clearly described blessings and curses that accompanied the sealing of the covenant. If you want to see the full expression of these for the Sinai covenant, look at Leviticus 26 and Deuteronomy 28. If the covenant was kept, remarkable blessings would follow; but if it was broken, the people would surely experience the blood curse they had called down upon themselves. We see proof of it here: The Israelite people have broken their covenant with Yahweh and the blood that trickled down their faces calls for retribution.

## The Creature Is Exalted

What happens when we try to meet our needs in our own way? First of all, we exalt the creature over the Creator. What image was this god of theirs made in? In the image of a bull, a creature of earth.[3] Why? And why do idolaters all over the earth make their gods to resemble various creatures? Well, if you believe you have to meet your own needs in your own way, what resource is left but the creation? You believe the transcendent, invisible God is of no use to you because you cannot manipulate him. So you try to harness the powers of the created world. You exalt the creation in hopes that you can persuade it to serve your needs. That is exactly what the Israelites did.

Why did they choose the bull? As we noted earlier, the bull was the chief idol in Egypt, so they fell back on what they had learned in their years of slavery. (Yahweh was attempting to

---

3. The Bible calls the image a "calf." In English, this refers to a baby animal. While the Hebrew term can be used in that way, it also encompasses a young animal with emerging sexual power. If the former sense is intended, then the Hebrew is mocking the supposed power of the bull idol. It is more likely that the second sense is intended.

deliver them from all the wrong ideas of their past, but they went right back to them!) Egypt worshiped the bull as a symbol of power. The bull can put his head down and butt anything out of his way. We want the ability to do that. We want to have brute force, and whenever we decide to serve our needs in our way, we start to deify brute force.

The bull was also a symbol of sexual potency. One of the heavy burdens for us humans is our mortality, which we realize especially as we begin to get older. Sexual potency is one way we can perpetuate ourselves. Really, the only living things that we leave behind us when we die are our descendants: our children and our grandchildren. So a bull symbolizes my ability to reproduce myself. If I can generate enough progeny, I can leave myself behind when I die. When we decide that we have to meet our needs our way, we exalt the creature and the power of the creature.

### Possessions Are Misused

A second thing that happens when we decide we have to meet our needs our way is that we misuse our possessions. Aaron commanded the Israelites to break the gold earrings off their ears. Where had that gold come from? It had come from Egypt. I doubt they had gold earrings when they were slaves. But God told them to ask the Egyptians for treasure when they left Egypt, and the Egyptians were so glad to see them go that they gladly complied. The Bible does not tell us why God instructed them to take the Egyptians' plunder, but in the end it is quite clear: so they would have resources with which to build the tabernacle. Now they use the possessions given them in trust to be used for Yahweh's glory, to exalt the Creator, to glorify the creature in hopes of fulfilling their immediate human needs.

## Needs Are Met Poorly

The third effect of taking matters into our own hands is that our needs get met very poorly. Compare that miserable golden bull to the tabernacle! Where is the variety of form, color, and texture? Where is the involvement of a variety of people's gifts in a variety of activities to glorify God? In fact, where is the involvement of the people at all? When we decide that we must meet our needs from within creation, the beautiful, talented, and powerful creatures of the world get exalted, while ordinary people are shut out. After giving Aaron their gold, the people were told in effect to sit down and shut up while they watched the professionals at work. The limit of their involvement was to shell out what they had.

Where did Aaron learn goldsmithing, anyway? He learned it in Egypt, of course. Molding and casting gold was highly skilled professional work, and now Aaron utilizes that skill in the service of what was not God, while the people merely watched. Whenever we decide we have to do it—whatever *it* may be—in our way and our time, you can mark it down that our possessions and our skills will be misused and our needs will be met poorly. At the same time, we will become the pawns of other people who prey on our fears, anxieties, and worries to reduce us in the end to mere paying spectators, not active participants.

Social commentators have long decried this as one of the greatest tragedies of television. We have all become couch potatoes, spectators watching other people "do their thing." No longer do we engage in silly little parades in our hometown, because we have seen the Rose Bowl Parade, and who can match that? Who wants to watch a bunch of straggling Boy Scouts walking down the street with the flag when, my goodness, we can see those bathing beauties in Southern California all decked out in roses?

## God-Given Boundaries Are Broken

The fourth thing that happens when we try to meet our own needs is that God-given boundaries are broken down. In the real world, there is a clear boundary between Yahweh and his creation. Paganism thinks it can dissolve that boundary. By making some aspect of the cosmos their deity, pagans hope to manipulate the cosmos and thus manipulate divine power. For this system to work, there cannot be boundaries between the sacred and profane. We are talking about the willful exercise of power, and power can admit no boundaries. Thus, pagans observe no boundary between parents and children: incest. They see no boundary between humans and animals: bestiality. Likewise, no boundaries around a husband and a wife: adultery. And no boundaries between males and males, or females and females: homosexuality.

What does God say to all of this? He says, "There is a boundary around you humans. You can't become your own god and you can't manipulate the true God. You can't make God do what you want." What are we saying when we insist that there are no boundaries in our world? "Nobody can tell me what to do with my life!"

How does that relate to the golden calf episode? After the calf had been unveiled, "the people sat down to eat and drink and rose up to play." What kind of play are we talking about here? It wasn't volleyball! In this case, the connotations of the English word *play* match those of the Hebrew word very closely. That is, it can refer to recreation, or to torture (the cat "played" with the mouse), or to sexual activity. In the context here, there is no doubt that the last connotation is intended. They engaged in sexual orgies. Why do orgies often accompany the worship of idols? Because sexual promiscuity is theological in nature! It is a very physical assertion of the theology of idolatry: god is this world and everything in it is god. There are no boundaries between divine power and ours, and there are no boundaries between my power and the power of nature. I make an idol in order to say, "I can bring god down into my world; I can break the boundary between me and god; I can drag god into this world and make him do what I want." We express that belief when we take the sexual power within us and break all the boundaries around it.

So it is not accidental that pagan worship often involves prostitution and bestiality. These are theological assertions. It is not accidental that when the boundary between you and God is broken down, the sexual boundaries are broken down too. The sexually promiscuous person says, "I can do what I want, when I want, where I want, because I am god in my life." The sexual immorality that we see in America today is not accidental. We have lost contact with God. We refuse to believe that there is a god who is beyond us and calls for our obedience—a god who cannot be manipulated or dragged into this world. I am not God, and neither are you. A firm boundary is fixed between us and him. No American wants to believe this. Our fiercely independent spirit says, "Nobody is going to tell me how to use the power that is mine."

That is where we are and where the Hebrew people were. The covenant between them and God had been broken; Yahweh's only covenant obligation after this moment is to destroy them. If he were to appear in their midst now, his very holiness would incinerate them. In order to communicate with God during this time, Moses must enter the Tent of Meeting, which is to be pitched far outside the camp (33:7). Their very attempt to bring God into their lives in their own strength and power in fact drove him away.

It is fascinating to me that the Israelites did not seem to understand what they were doing. In 32:1, the translations all have the people saying, "Come make us gods that will go before us." But the same Hebrew word can be translated as God or gods, depending on the context. I think it is very probable that what they intended to say to Aaron was: "Come, make us God."

To read the dialogue at face value, it appears that the Israelites still intended to worship the Lord, but in their own way. They were going to worship him in the way that seemed most appropriate to them. This seems confirmed by what Aaron says in 32:5, "Aaron made a proclamation and he said, 'Tomorrow is a feast to the Lord.'" They could not see that there was any problem in worshiping a bull figure, a part of creation, as if it were the great "I AM."

Tragically, again and again in the Old Testament, people paganize the worship of God and do not even realize it. We dare not be very harsh in condemning the Israelites, however, for it is also true of the church in America today. We drag God down to our level, we make him a mere image of what he has created. You say, "We don't have any statues of God in our church." Perhaps not, but we make him something small and useful; we make him our servant. Why do we go to church? So that God will bless us. Why do we have devotions? To get rid of some pain. ("I have had my devotions for seven weeks straight, and I still have this pain in my back. Now God, the only reason I have been doing these devotions—and they are a pain in the neck—was to get rid of the pain in the back. Either you relieve the pain or forget any more devotions.")

If we wonder why our lives are dull, dry, and empty, it is often because we have made God an idol. We have made God our helper and servant. We have expected God to do our bidding. Again and again in the Old Testament, the downfall of God's people was not so much that they turned away from Yahweh to worship some other god. Usually, it happened because they tried to worship the true God and their artificial gods at the same time.

One of the most tragic passages in all the Bible is found in Ezekiel 23:38–39. There God says, "You sacrificed my children, the children that I gave you, to idols, and then with bloody hands you walk up the hill to the temple and lift those hands in praise to me." And what about us? We are sacrificing children by the millions to our convenience and our unbridled sexual license. We are sacrificing more children in a year by abortion than all our troops who died in the Second World War.

But not only that, we are sacrificing our living children too. "I don't have time for you, kid. I have to work in order to support this big house we have. You're not worth my time, child." Oh, we sacrifice them. "I was a lousy football player, but my kid is going to be a great football player. Stop reading that book and get out there and kick that football." Or, "I was never popular and attractive when I was a girl, so my eight-year-old darling, I will deck you out like a godless pop star." We sacrifice them to our idols. Then we go to church to praise God and wonder why it is all so dull, dead, and empty.

That is what they were doing, "Oh, we are worshiping the Lord." Yes, they thought they were worshiping him. But they were worshiping him according to their needs. They were worshiping him in a way that would make him accessible to them for their purposes. But God says, "I am the Lord, and you are the servants, and I will determine how you worship me." God forbid that we do the very thing that the Hebrew people did and never know we are doing it.

## Questions for Personal Study or Discussion

1. In what way is a new Christian like a house that's swept clean (Matt 12:43–45)?

2. On Mount Sinai, God gave Moses a set of construction plans—for what structure? Why?

3. From which of the twelve Hebrew tribes were priests to be chosen? Were Moses and Aaron members of this tribe? Was Jesus (see his genealogy in Matthew 1)?

4. Why does the book of Exodus repeat and summarize so many things—lists of laws, construction plans, and so on? What technical name do Bible scholars give to this writing method?

5. Review the four needs that Dr. Oswalt cites for Israel to have such an elaborate worship structure and ritual. How well do you think Israel's worship patterns met these needs?

6. How well do you think your own congregation's worship patterns meet these four needs?

7. What are some of the ways Dr. Oswalt mentioned that we "paganize" God? What other ways can you think of?

8. Think of some times when you waited for God longer than you thought possible, and in the end he fulfilled his promise to you.

CHAPTER 12

# The Revelation of His Presence
## —Part 2

## Response to the Golden Calf Incident (32:1–34:35)

Anyone who does not understand the importance of the covenant might think that what Aaron and the people did was just a little faux pas, a slip-up. All they did was make one idol, and it was a first-time offense, after all. Surely there was no reason for God to be angry. Surely, he could say, "We'll just overlook it this time."

But what happened here was not a little faux pas. The people had sworn a blood oath not to recognize any other gods and not to make idols. Now they had done those very things. Their bond is broken and must be put back to rights. We tend to say, "But their oath was just words. Words are not things that can be broken." That is just where we are wrong. We have lost a vital understanding that the Hebrews and many other ancient people had. When words are spoken, they bring something into existence that now has an identity of its own. Every one of us has had the experience of saying something in haste and afterward wishing we could unsay it. But we cannot. Our words are out there and will be out there until the end of time. Something has to be said or done to make the situation right. It cannot just be ignored.[1]

Furthermore, this was not just a little idol. By forbidding them to make idols, Yahweh took a giant step toward correcting the false understanding of reality that had come to infect the whole world: He is not the world! But so long as people think they can capture deity in the forms of this world, they are never going to learn that essential fact. I suspect that Egypt has much to answer for right here. In Egyptian theology you could say that a god is invisible and visible at the same time. The beauty of that idea is that all things are continuous. Something can be so and not so at the same time. The principle of transcendence, in which the I AM is completely other than that which he has created, denies that silliness with vehemence. Because God is not the world, he cannot be represented by any of the forms of this world. I suspect that Aaron had no problem making the idol because he reasoned that Moses was worshiping the invisible Yahweh on the mountain and he, Aaron, was simply helping the people worship the visible Yahweh down in the valley. But Moses knew you cannot have it both ways. God cannot be part of the world and not part of the world at the same time. As a result, as we will see, Moses' anger over the event made Yahweh's anger look rather mild.

## Moses' Intercession

What happened on the mountain was most significant. Yahweh said that Moses' people, whom Moses had led out of Egypt, had now corrupted their way. If Moses would just leave him alone, God would destroy these people and raise up a new nation in

---

1. The Hebrew word that is translated "word" actually connotes "thing," or "event" as well. It makes the point that a word has an independent existence of its own.

Moses' name. What is that about? They are not Moses' people, but Yahweh's. And what does Moses' leaving Yahweh alone have to do with it? Yahweh was perfectly within his rights to descend from the mountain and consume those idolatrous people. Just a few weeks before, they had stood in his presence and sworn complete loyalty to him. They had said in effect, "May God strike me dead if I ever break this covenant." So God was not merely within his rights, he was legally obligated to destroy them. Why should he ask Moses to leave him alone? And how could Moses' not leaving him alone change anything?

To answer these questions, we need to look at Moses' response. First of all, he says, "Yahweh, these are not my people; they are yours." How easily he could have taken God's cue and said, "Yes, they are my people and look how they have treated me after all I've done for them." But he knew better.

Then he says, "If you do this, the Egyptians will think you are just one more of the gods." Egyptian myth said that the gods will treat you nicely as long as it suits them, but just do something they don't like and they'll destroy you. Clearly, Moses had learned something about the character of Yahweh, about his unearthly faithfulness. Maybe no one else in Israel yet realized that Yahweh was different, but Moses had.

Moses could have rationalized that since he was a descendant of Abraham, God would still be keeping his promise to the patriarch if the people were not called the children of Jacob but the children of Moses. He did not. God had made promises to a long line of Hebrew patriarchs about their descendants, and to wipe out all the children of Jacob except for one representative of the tribe of Levi simply would not do. Moses was saying that Yahweh is not simply just; he is true.

In response, Yahweh agreed with Moses and suggested that he, Moses, should go down and talk to the people. This is not a picture of a raging, roaring, out-of-control God with a cowering Moses pleading for him to control himself, and God slowly backs down. In fact, I would suggest that the conversation is actually a test of Moses. Does Moses understand who Yahweh really is, or will he agree with the suggestion that his people have embarrassed him and deserve to be punished? (Many ministers have succumbed to that temptation.) Does Moses understand who Yahweh really is, or will he accept the offer to become the new father of the nation?

If this conversation was a test, as I believe, then Moses passed it with flying colors. After all the ways in which these people had already failed him, Moses still bears them and God in his heart, which is exactly what Yahweh was inviting him to do. Remember that every test is an opportunity to succeed. God did not want Abraham to sacrifice Isaac, but he had to know how Abraham really felt about God. In the same way here, Yahweh did not want Moses to say, "Go get 'em, God!" Rather, he wanted Moses to say, as he did, "You are not a hair-trigger god who is only concerned with defending his honor. You are a God who keeps his promises, even when there is no legal reason to do so. Your faithfulness is not limited by your people's unfaithfulness."

I believe this is why Yahweh so quickly lays his anger aside: Moses understood that our God remembers. He remembers his promises, he remembers his covenant, and he remembers his faithfulness. Though he may be justly angry at our sins, justly furious at our fickleness and our failures, he also remembers that our names are written on his hands. He is that kind of God, and Moses knew it as well as he did.

## Moses' Reaction

What happened then? When Moses actually saw what was going on in the Israelites' camp, his anger made Yahweh's seem small in comparison. He hurled to the ground the tablets on which God had inscribed the Ten Commandments, smashing them. This symbolized the breaking of the covenant, but it also spoke of a monumental anger. Then he threw the golden idol into the fire, softening it. He took a sledge hammer and smashed it to dust. Then he flung the dust into the people's drinking water and made them drink it. That gold would never be used to make an idol nor to profane the tabernacle of Yahweh! That is anger. Sometimes we are much too passive in the face of evil; and we need to take a page from Moses' book.

What happened next carries an important lesson for us. Moses asked who was on Yahweh's side, and members of the tribe of Levi, Moses' own tribe, responded. Then he told them to go through the camp and kill their brother, their companion, and their neighbor. They did so, killing about three thousand men. Why did Moses specify that they kill brother, companion, and neighbor? I can only offer suggestions because the text is so terse. I believe that since Moses' brother Aaron made the idol and proclaimed the festival, people from the tribe of Levi were probably the ringleaders in what took place. We can only guess how much more trouble there might have been if those people had been allowed to live. It is so in our own lives. There comes a time to be ruthless with sin. We dare not coddle it or make a place for it, any more than we would treat cancer cells in that way. This is what Jesus meant when, using Semitic hyperbole, he said that if your eye causes you to sin you should tear it out (Mark 9:47). I sense that Moses gained a new appreciation for the seriousness of what the people had done after seeing it at firsthand. Before he came down the mountain, Yahweh's report was disturbing enough, and Moses was primarily concerned that Yahweh's name not be slandered. But when Moses saw what had taken place, it was as though he suddenly understood the gravity of it.

After Moses had smashed the idol, and had supervised the killing of the ringleaders, he recognized that those things were still not enough to blot out the full effect of what had been done. This level of sin would require atonement, or covering. So Moses went back up the mountain saying that he would try to make that atonement (32:30). How he thought he would do that is not clear, but it appears that he thought he could persuade God on the basis of his own standing with God. When he arrived back on the mountain top, he told Yahweh, "Alas, this people have sinned a great sin. They have made for themselves gods of gold. But now, if you will, forgive them. If not, please blot me out of your book that you have written" (32:31–32).

One of my teachers, a dear friend, has suggested that Moses was offering his life on behalf of the people. Unfortunately, I cannot see how this text is saying that. It seems to me that Moses thought he could engage in a little divine arm-twisting: "Please forgive them for my sake, Lord. But if you won't do that, just kill me along with them." Yahweh's response confirms this understanding. Rather mildly, he replied that the only person who was going to get blotted out of the book was the sinner. So Moses should get up off the ground and continue leading the people to the Promised Land. What this incident says to me is that sometimes we can forget our place in the order of things and suppose that we are important enough to cut deals with God. If we do, though, God puts us back in our places.

However we understand what Moses intended, his essential conviction was correct: Sin requires atonement. But this leaves an important question unanswered: If Moses could not cover his people's sin, yet God forgave them, where did the atonement come from? We who live after Christ know the answer: Forgiveness in any time is made possible by the death of Christ, the second Person of the Trinity.

### The Resolution of the Issue

Chapters 33–34 show us how the incident of the golden calf was finally resolved. Yahweh begins by saying that he will keep his promise to give the people the Promised Land, but he himself cannot go with them lest he consume them (33:1–6). Moses' response to this is surely one of the great affirmations in Scripture. (Again, we see how much Moses had learned.) He replied that if God could not go with them, then they would stay where they were. The desert with Yahweh was better than the Promised Land without him (33:14–15). Moses understood the whole point toward which the book of Exodus is driving: Salvation comes when a person experiences the unhindered presence of Yahweh in his or her life. Circumstances may be better or worse—we may be in a desert or enjoying the good things of Canaan—but our circumstances are meaningless without the reality of God moving through our lives.

God seemed to be waiting for a response like that, waiting to see if anyone understood what he had been trying to teach these people. On the basis of Moses' affirmation of faith, God said that he knew Moses by name and would go with them. How often in the history of biblical faith has the faithful response of just one person given God cause to extend his blessings to hundreds and thousands of people who did not deserve those blessings! The prophet Ezekiel suggests that the absence of such a person finally exposed God's people to exile, which had been held off for hundreds of years (Ezek 22:30).

Moses was so thrilled by Yahweh's promises that he requested an even deeper experience of God's reality; he asked that he might see the glory of God (33:18). Yahweh's response is very instructive. He said that he would show Moses his goodness. So what is the difference? Glory denotes God's essence, while goodness is his character. Moses seems to have been looking for an ineffable experience of Yahweh's very essence, an experience like Paul's being caught up to the third heaven, for which there really are no words (2 Cor 12:2–3). But Yahweh gently reminded Moses that a barrier is fixed between the essence of the Creator and the essence of the created. Surely that is what he meant when he said that no one can see his face and live.

So what did Moses experience? We are told that Moses saw God's back, but we have not one word about what his back looked like! Rather, the Exodus narrator describes the holy character that God longs to share with us. The description in 34:6–7 explains what happened in 34:8 and following, where the covenant is reaffirmed. But notice that it is a unilateral reaffirmation. The Hebrew people had broken the covenant; God was obliged to destroy them. Yet unilaterally he said, "Bring me two more stones, Moses, and I will write the Ten Commandments on these stones again."

In other words, God said, "I am going to keep my covenant though I have no need to, no legal obligation to do so. I am going to keep my covenant regardless of their sin." The covenant as given in chapter 34 is even more specific about idolatry and true worship, as though God is saying, "Apparently, I was not specific enough in the previous statement. I did not give enough specific examples of how not making an idol and not having any other gods before me was supposed to work. So here they are."

But look carefully at the message Moses heard. The verbal revelation explains what it is about Yahweh that makes such a reaffirmation of the covenant possible. "And the Lord passed before him and proclaimed, 'Yahweh, Yahweh God, merciful and gracious; slow to anger and abounding in faithful love and truth; keeping faithful love to thousands, forgiving iniquity, transgression and sin....'" (34:6–7). This description of the character of God is the most frequently quoted in the Old Testament, appearing six times as a quotation and about a dozen more times in allusions. God's justice and majesty, his holiness and his righteousness, are all true and clearly taught; but the thing that captured the Israelites' imagination, the quality that stood out to them as the unique character of Yahweh was this: He loves us even though we do not deserve it, so he does not punish at the first offense. He is compassionate with our weakness and patient with our failings. These are the things that distinguish this God from every other so-called god. These qualities allow him to enter into covenant with obstinate, fallen people like us.

The promise says that his faithful love (*hesed*) is shown to thousands. The quotation in Deuteronomy 7:9 makes it explicit that it is "to a thousand generations of them that love him." This is very important for understanding the rest of verse 7: "...but who will not make the guilty innocent, bringing the iniquity of the fathers on the children and the children's children to the third and the fourth generation." It is a mark of our fallenness that we skim right across the stunning affirmations of verses 6 and 7a and land heavily on this statement. We say, "What a cruel God, to punish innocent children for what their parents have done!" But look at the previous statement. If you will faithfully keep Yahweh's covenant, through the power of the Holy Spirit made available to you through the atonement of Christ, the effect in your family will be truly endless. God's blessing will extend to a thousand generations. On the other hand, if you choose to live in sin, defying the grace of God, presuming on his forgiving grace, he will limit the effects to only three or four generations. What a good God we have!

But why should the children suffer any effects of their parents' sin at all? Again, look at the context: great news, Yahweh forgives iniquity, transgression, and sin. Great! So I will live in pleasurable sin for a few years and then, at the last minute, repent and receive his forgiveness. Then everything will be fine. No, it won't. Such a scheme forgets one great principle of this creation Yahweh has made: cause and effect. God is glad to forgive. He is merciful, and he is glad to be merciful, but he is still a God of justice. His mercy does not alter the consequences of sin.

An old illustration still makes the point clearly. Suppose I drive nails into my wife's beautiful desk and then come to my senses and beg her forgiveness. Suppose she graciously forgives me, and I pull the nails out. Will the holes close up because I am forgiven? Of course not! The nails may be gone, but the holes remain.

So God says, "John, if you do a horrible thing and commit adultery against your wife, I will forgive you if you repent. I will restore your relationship with me. But John, don't think for one moment that the effects of what you did are not going to touch your children, your grandchildren, and your great-grandchildren. Don't assume that because I am a God of mercy and grace, you can sin with impunity. Don't suppose that you can sin however you please, in the knowledge that when you are done, you can repent and I will forgive you. It's not that simple." We need to know not only that God is merciful and kind but that this is also a world of justice. If we sin, there will be consequences in our own lives and those of our descendants.

# Doing Things God's Way (35:1–40:38)

*What God's Way Was Intended to Show*

This second description of the tabernacle and its service provides a good opportunity to consider what God was saying in the design and construction of the complex. First of all, notice the wonderful variety in textures, colors, and materials. There was linen, wool, leather, wood, bronze, silver, gold, and jewels. There were vivid colors of white, blue, red, and purple. There were plaited cords, plain fabric, and embroidered fabric. While there have been differing attempts to explain the significance of each of these, the overall point is unmistakable: Yahweh's world is one of breathtaking variety and beauty. As Isaiah says, Yahweh's glory fills the earth (Isa 6:3). Yahweh celebrated that variety and beauty in the tabernacle that he instructed his people to build in the wilderness. He was also celebrating the multiple senses that he has given to each of us, especially the visual and the tactile. He was saying that he reveals himself in all these things, so all that we are and have can be brought into his service.

The plan of the complex was also significant. The outer enclosure spoke of the barrier that must forever distinguish the Creator from the created. We cannot obliterate that distinction; we cannot become God. God may become us—indeed, he did—but we cannot become him. That truth is further emphasized by the three veils that bar the way to the inner sanctum. There is one at the opening of the court, another at the opening of the tent, and yet another before the covenant box. They were all beautifully embroidered, representing something of the stunning beauty of the Creator and his inaccessibility from our side of the equation.

Inside the first veil, the first sight was the Great Altar, which tells us that there is no forgiveness of sin without the shedding of blood. Sin is an insurmountable barrier to any fellowship between us and our Creator; so until something is done about it, there is no way into the divine presence. But the altar also says that if a suitable substitute could be found, then the sin could be covered over, the broken law satisfied, and access would be possible.

Here the role of the priests, especially the high priest, was vital. For here our need of a mediator is demonstrated. If we are to stand before Yahweh and live, then someone must represent us—someone whose holiness is unsullied, someone who figuratively carries us on his shoulders and in his heart. The beauty of the high priest's robes, chestpiece, ephod, and turban emphasizes the wonder of what Yahweh had planned for us in the ministry of the Mediator, Jesus Christ. The writer of the book of Hebrews makes this ministry very clear when he speaks of the perfect high priest who brings to God a perfect sacrifice, namely himself.

Beyond the altar stood the laver, where the priests washed. This emphasizes the truth that substitution, with its overtones of a change in our legal status from criminal to innocent, does not completely express what God wants to do for us. He not only requires a change in our legal status but also a change in our condition—from dirty to clean and from defiled to pure. Both changed status and changed character are required if we are to survive the presence of the holy God. This speaks of the regenerating and sanctifying work of the Holy Spirit.

With the altar and the laver behind us, we are ready to pass through the second veil, into Yahweh's living room, as it were. Here the blessings of fellowship with him become more real and tangible. On the right is the table where the bread of the presence was displayed. In pagan temples, food was placed on such a table for the god to eat. The apostle Paul refers to this as food offered to idols (1 Cor 8). After having been offered to the gods, it was then sold to the public. In contrast, the table in the tabernacle seems to represent the kind of fellowship meal that the peace offering represented. God was present to have communion with the reconciled offerer. There were twelve loaves on the table, one for each tribe. God invited each of the tribes to his table for fellowship. So the pagans had it exactly backwards: We do not provide bread for our God to eat; rather, he gives himself to us, saying "I am the Bread of Life."

A lampstand stood on the left side of the Holy Place. It was shaped like a tree with an almond bud on the end of each branch. The lamps were flat bowls holding olive oil. There was a flattened place in the rim of each bowl, and on that flattened place a wick lay with one end in the oil and the other hanging out to be lighted. The pagan temples had something similar as a light for the god to see by; but in God's house, this seven-flamed lampstand represented the light that God brings into a dark world. Again, it was Jesus who said, "I am the light of the world" (John 8:12).

The third veil hung across the back of this room. In front of it stood an incense altar. Across the ancient world, incense was burned in temples—perhaps originally to blot out the myriad smells of the sacrificial activity that took place in the courts outside. But here in the tabernacle, burning incense symbolized the prayers of the saints, which God delights to receive (e.g., Rev 5:8).

In a pagan temple the innermost cell of the building was the place where the god himself or herself lived in the form of the idol. How very different was the situation in the tabernacle and the later temple. There was no idol behind the third veil in the Most Holy Place, only a box—a remarkable box, to be sure, plated with gold and hovered over by golden cherubim. In the box were the tablets of the covenant and (initially at least) Aaron's rod and a bowl of manna. But the covenant was the most important and enduring. There could be no idol here, because Yahweh is not of this world and cannot be captured in any of the forms of this world. That also means that he cannot be manipulated through any of the forms of this world. He cannot be moved through magical rituals or incantations. Instead, he comes to us and offers to bind himself to us in a covenant. The only way to relate to him is to accept his gracious offer of himself in trust and surrender, believing his promises and staking our lives upon his trustworthiness. As we live our lives in obedience to his covenant, we begin to learn who he is and what he is like, because the terms of our covenant with him reflect his own character. So it was that the Israelites believed God was uniquely present above the cherubim that shielded the box.

However, the covenant was broken. The tablets within that box cried out for justice. The very thing that defined the Hebrew people stood over against them, condemning them. So once each year, the high priest sprinkled blood onto the cover of the box. (There seems to have been a wordplay here, for the cover was the place where the blood "covered" their sin, preventing the voice of the broken covenant from reaching to Yahweh above.) Yet how can the blood of bulls and goats cover our sin, as Micah asked? Even our own children's blood could not cover our sin. But we are being prepared to hear the Lamb of God proclaim, "This is my blood, shed for you and for many, for the remission of sins" (Matt 26:28).

### The Results of Doing Things God's Way

**General participation.** There is a dramatic difference between worship of the golden calf and worship according to God's instructions. First of all, Yahweh mandated general, not limited, participation in worship. Everybody had something to give—not just the people with gold earrings! You see, when we try to obtain God's blessings our way, we decide what is worthy to be given in worship and a lot of people are left out. "If you do not have gold earrings, forget it; you have no part in this." But when we worship God's way, everybody has something to give. Do you have some gold? Good. Give it. Some silver? Good. Give it. Some bronze? Good. Give it. Some acacia wood? Good. Give it. Some yarn? Good, give it. Some colored dyes? Good. Give it. Anything else? Give that too. Everybody has something to give when you honor God in God's way.

Not only did everyone have something to give, everyone had something to do. Rather than sitting by while the religious professional constructed an idol to capture the essence of deity in an earthly form, many different people were involved in expressing the wonderful symbols of Yahweh's gracious presence among his people. Bezalel and Oholiab were the designated leaders, but they were also teachers (35:34), gifted to train many other men and women to whom God had given a variety of skills that could be used in a variety of ways. There were engravers, designers, embroiderers, and weavers, to name a few (35:35). The community's participation in constructing the tabernacle was general, not limited. So it is in God's kingdom today. It is so easy for us to say that if you cannot preach, sing, teach, or don't have a lot of money, you will just have to be a spectator. But that is not true. Every one of us is made in the image of God, which means that each person's contribution is valuable, even if we can only sweep floors or change light bulbs. Everyone has something to give.

**Participation is voluntary, not coerced.** The worship participation of God's people is also voluntary and not coerced. Notice Exodus 35:21: They came, "everyone whose heart was stirred, and everyone whose spirit was willing, and they brought the LORD's offering" (NKJV). The people did not say, "We had better do this or Aaron is going to get us." Nor was it, "We had better do this or he won't be able to make a god for us." I am confident that the experiences of the preceding chapters had something to do with this attitude. "Great Scott, we are still alive after what we did. How can I express my thanks that God has spared me? I have some stuff here I want to give to the Lord." You see, when we think that God owes us something, our giving will be stingy and tight-fisted. When we know that we owe God everything, our giving is generous.

**Participation is spiritually motivated.** Their worship participation was spiritually motivated, not externally prompted. We noted above that Bezalel, the master craftsman, was filled by the Holy Spirit to design and construct the tabernacle. But notice what is said of the people: Their spirits were willing. That is, something from within them motivated them to be a part of this great undertaking. How different this is from Psalm 78:8, which says the people's "hearts were not established and their spirits were not faithful to God." True worshipers are people whose spirits rely on God and who thus could be relied on by God. They were not moved by the thought that they could induce God to do something for them as a result of their giving; rather, they gave because of their own spirit's desire to take part in the Spirit's work. This resonance between human spirit and divine Spirit evoked a desire to be part of what God was doing. So the motivator for giving here was the Spirit of the Lord. The people's spirits were in line with his Spirit.

**Participation had to be restrained.** What is the result of that kind of motivation? The people had to be restrained! They were giving so much stuff for the tabernacle construction that the craftsmen came to Moses and said, "You've got to tell them to stop.

We have more than we can use" (36:5–7). Would you like to see your pastor faint dead away? Just tell him that while you have been tithing for some time, you just feel that it is not enough and you want to give more to God's work. Say, "God has been letting me keep 90 percent of his money. I have got to give him more to tell him how much I love him. I have got to give him more to tell him how grateful I am for what he has done for me—to say thank you, thank you, thank you." I guarantee you that he will fall down in a dead faint, because most us give the very minimum that we think we can, and our pastors have to wrestle with that fact constantly.

Grace changes our spiritual perspective. If you see someone who drops a nickel into the offering and then expects God to do a handstand, you are looking at someone who has never really experienced the grace of God. But if you find someone who just cannot give enough, you are looking at someone who has known that they were dead and are now alive, they were empty and are now full, they were lost and are now found. These are the people who say, "O God, there is not enough time or stuff in the world to thank you adequately for what you have done for me."

Too often we forget that everything we have is a gift from God. That happened to the Israelites. They were slaves, paupers—they had nothing. But God said, "Look, the night before you are ready to leave Egypt, I want you to go to your Egyptian neighbor and say, 'Do you have any gold or silver you'd like to give me?'" And the Egyptians, having had more than enough of the plagues brought upon them by the Israelites' God, said, "Sure, take anything you want. Just GO!" So the Israelites went out of Egypt millionaires. What do you think they said then? I am afraid it went something like this: "Boy, oh boy, it is about time that I got a little reward for all my suffering and hard work. This is all mine, and I am going to use it exactly as I choose."

Like the Israelites, we had nothing. Everything we have is a gift. None of us brought any possessions with us on the day we were born, and none of us will take anything with us on the day we die. Every earthly possession is a gift from God.

**Specifications as Yahweh commanded.** The specifications were as Yahweh commanded, not as Aaron decided. That phrase "as Yahweh commanded" resounds throughout the final section, Exodus 35–40. However, it is especially prominent in chapters 39–40, which speak of the actual erection of the tabernacle complex. By my count, the phrase occurs no less than sixteen times in those two chapters. Clearly, Moses was trying to make a point. They did not do things as they wished; they did not do things the way they had learned in Egypt; and they did not imitate the Canaanites, in whose land they were going to live. They did as Yahweh commanded. It should be pointed out that there is some evidence that the Egyptians may have had moveable shrines of a similar set-up/take-down construction as the tabernacle. Furthermore, the general layout of court, outer room, and inner room is similar to that of Canaanite temples. So the fact that the construction was "as Yahweh commanded" did not rule out God's using ideas, materials, and patterns that might be familiar to the Israelites. But it was his choice that made the difference. They were not doing what they wanted or what they thought best in order to manipulate divine power to supply their needs. They were allowing I AM to define their needs and how best to meet those needs. That makes all the difference. The issue is not whether we should use other people's ideas, methods, and patterns in accomplishing God's work. Rather, the issue is whether we have surrendered our desires, our needs, our ways into God's hands so that we can hear how he wants to accomplish his work in us as well as through us.

**Results: Blessing and Divine presence.** The first result of their obedience was blessing. When Moses saw what had been done, he blessed the people (39:43). How different this was from when he came down the mountain to see the calf! As the representative of the broken covenant, Moses could only pronounce the covenant curses over them. So it must always be with our attempts to capture God's power for ourselves. This is simply a breach of the constraints of reality. God's power is not ours to capture, and never will be. We may as well seize the ends of a live electric wire to try to get its power for ourselves. The result will be death, as it was for the idolaters at the foot of Sinai. If we do not use electricity within the parameters of reality, it will kill us, and the same is true with God. That is not God's desire. His desire is to bless us, and that desire is so strong that if we meet the most minimum of requirements, he will do so.

This is what the prophet Jonah was not ready to accept when God sent him to the city of Nineveh to preach repentance. The Assyrians were bad people. They were the terrible enemies of Israel. Surely, Jonah thought, God would not relent from the destruction they so richly deserved just because they repented one time. But that is all it took to change the curse into blessing, and so it was here in Exodus. Even though the covenant had been tragically broken, if they would just turn back to do things God's way, he would gladly bless them.

That brings us to the greatest result of all: the very presence of God in the midst of the camp. "And the glory of God filled the tabernacle so that no one could go in there." God's presence was so real, so vital, so powerful, that one just had to stand back in awe and say, "God is here. God is here." Here is the climax of the whole book of Exodus. From slaves using their hands to build the houses of Pharaoh and his gods, the Israelites became redeemed men and women in whose very presence the Presence chose to dwell, using their hands to build his dwelling. Out of bondage, theological darkness and alienation, they came into the very arms of God.

This is our inheritance as people redeemed by Christ: We can know the presence of God in the very midst of our lives each day. We can commune with him "mouth to mouth" as Moses did. Would it not be wonderful if people were to look at our faces, as the Hebrews looked at Moses when he had been in the presence of God, and say, "Turn it off. Turn it off. It is too bright." The glory of God was so evident in Moses' life and character that no one could not miss it.

Oh, that such a thing might be true of us! The glory of God has come into our lives. We have surrendered our way and our purposes and our plans to God, and we say instead, "Your way, your purposes, your plans." So now God's glory has filled the tabernacle. His glory has filled our lives and nobody can miss it. Such is the inheritance of all who have experienced the exodus.

## Questions for Personal Study or Discussion

1.  Which of the Ten Commandments did the Israelites break while Moses was on the mountain? Why was this such a serious breach in their relationship with God?

2.  Review the conversation between God and Moses about what the Israelites had done (Ex 32:7–14). Underline arguments that Moses puts forward that show that he is acting as an intercessor (go-between) for the Israelites instead of trying to protect his personal interests.

3.  Consider how Jesus interceded in prayer for his disciples, and then rewrite Moses' arguments as Jesus might have made them on behalf of the Twelve.

4.  Consider how your pastor intercedes in prayer for you, and then rewrite these arguments as your pastor might make them on your behalf.

5.  Review Dr. Oswalt's main points in the section titled "The Results of Doing Things God's Way." How well does the worship life of your congregation produce these results? What can you do personally to promote these results?

6.  Review the three problems that God delivered his people from in the book of Exodus. Has Jesus delivered you from those as well? How?

7.  Dr. Oswalt says that when God's "glory has filled our lives and nobody can miss it," we have made a genuine exodus

out of our old way of life. In what ways is he wanting to fill your life more fully today? Pray that God's Spirit will reign in your life, today and always.